Two into One:

Relating in Christian Marriage

Joyce Huggett

InterVarsity Press
Downers Grove
Illinois 60515

© *Joyce Huggett 1981*

*Printed in America by InterVarsity Press, Downers Grove, Illinois, with permission
from Universities and Colleges Christian Fellowship, Leicester, England.*

*InterVarsity Press is the book-publishing division of Inter-Varsity Christian Fellowship,
a student movement active on campus at hundreds of universities, colleges
and schools of nursing. For information about local and regional activities, write
IVCF, 233 Langdon St., Madison, WI 53703.*

*Distributed in Canada through InterVarsity Press, 1875 Leslie St., Unit 10,
Don Mills, Ontario M3B 2M5, Canada.*

*Unless otherwise stated, quotations from the Bible are from the Revised Standard Version,
copyrighted 1946, 1952, © 1971, 1973, by the Division of Christian Education, National
Council of the Churches of Christ in the USA, and used by permission.*

Cover photograph: Robert McKendrick

ISBN 0-87784-614-6

Printed in the United States of America

Library of Congress Cataloging in Publication Data

Huggett, Joyce, 1937-
   Two into one.

   Includes bibliographical references.
    1. Marriage—Moral and religious aspects.
I. Title.
BV835.H83   248.8'4   81-19284
ISBN 0-87784-614-6   AACR2

17	16	15	14	13	12	11	10	9	8	7	6	5	4	3	2	1
95	94	93	92	91	90	89	88	87	86	85	84	83	82	81		

Abbreviations

Bible references which are not taken from the
Revised Standard Version are quoted with the
following abbreviations:

AV	*Authorized Version (King James'),* 1611
GNB	*Good News Bible,* 1976
JB	*Jerusalem Bible,* 1966
NIV	*New International Version,* 1979

Preface

Sixteen years ago my husband and I left suburbia to train for full time ministry in the Anglican Church. When you wear a dog collar, or are married to a man who wears one, people assume that you are competent to steer them through all kinds of choppy waters.

For years, therefore, Christian couples have poured out their marital problems to us. Fractured marriages hurt. We sought to alleviate the pain, to offer guidance, to give support, but in the early days we were well aware that we gave little more than compassion, superficial platitudes and the cold comfort, 'We'll pray for you.'

The conviction grew that we should equip ourselves to give more adequate help, and so we found ourselves training in order to discover the dynamics of relationships. We even examined our own impoverished marriage.

As we participated in marriage-growth work of various kinds over a period of years, three certainties took root: that Christian marriage contains the potential for bringing wholeness to the persons creating the partnership, that marriage as God designed it is about freedom, growth and security, and that hard work is an essential ingredient of satisfying relationships.

Many people these days are involved in the vital work of mending broken marriages, though most of us would agree that of the two kinds of healing, prevention and cure, the former is to be preferred.

This book, therefore, is about prevention, planning, looking ahead. We are not primarily addressing the middle-aged, those who, like us, have made their mistakes. We are not primarily concerned even with young couples with children, though we hope some of the insights might prove helpful to married people in all phases of life. Our main concern is for newly-weds and those who are preparing to be married, whose expectations of married life submitted to God are high, who are determined to create the best marriage ever. Some chapters are written specifically for married couples (*e.g.* 9, 10), others are more general.

We are not offering a blue-print for a happy marriage. That would be foolish, for each marriage is as unique as the couple who unite to become 'one flesh'. Neither do we offer a guarantee of unmitigated joy. Few couples succeed in every aspect of their relationship. Rather we have attempted to blaze a trail which we believe will enable you to avoid some of the traps which have ensnared others. We aim to provide signposts which you may follow on a journey whose delights are found as much in the travelling as in the arriving.

We consider that this book is not so much something to be read, as preparation to be done. You will gain maximum help from it if you involve yourselves in the questions posed. If you lived in our parish we should invite you to attend a mini-conference with other couples and encourage you to work at some of the assignments there and then. A book is second best to personal encounter, but we offer this with the prayer that it will enable you, as a couple, to clarify your goals for a Christ-centred marriage which is the Christian ideal.

Christian marriage involves two people becoming one. In that my husband and I have discussed each chapter, and even changed our life-style in the light of discoveries unearthed in the writing of the book, we have written it together. The hand which holds the pen is feminine but the breadth of thinking embraces both halves of our partnership as well as the contributions of friends and counsellors. The learning never comes to an end and that realization excites us as we move towards our silver wedding anniversary. Have we written a book on marriage, I wonder, or is it the book which is writing us?

1 Excited by Marriage

Mention of marriage produces a mixture of reactions. Some people, like Sir Winston Churchill, are excited by it: 'It's the best thing I ever did in my life.' Others, like C. S. Lewis, relish marital intimacy:

> For those few years H. and I feasted on love; every mode of it – solemn and merry, romantic and realistic, sometimes as dramatic as a thunderstorm, sometimes as comfortable as putting on your soft slippers. No cranny of heart or body remained unsatisfied.[1]

And many, like Sheldon Vanauken, express satisfaction:

> Every year on our anniversary we said, 'If we're not more deeply in love next year, we shall have failed.' But we were: a deeper inloveness, more close, more dear. She in me and I in her: the co-inherence of lovers. And every year we would drink to the future in the old toast: 'If it's half as good as the half we've known, here's *Hail!* to the rest of the road.'[2]

But not everyone applauds marriage. Some people assert that there is something seriously wrong with marriage itself. Journalists high-light the stultifying effect which sick marriages produce: 'I can't stand this idea of being one with the person you marry, it's so destructive.'[3] Humanist thinkers are in the forefront in offering alternative structures to the 'strait-jacket' of life-long partnership. And even some Christians are cynical about marriage. It was summed up for me by a voice shrieking down the telephone recently, 'Marriage is nothing more than a sick joke. I've yet to meet a happily married couple.' Discussions about marriage today arouse conflicting and confused feelings.

But life consists of more than feelings and it is imperative that we place the facts about marriage alongside the feelings. As Christians who believe that the Bible contains authoritative counsel from the Creator of life, the author of interpersonal relationships, Almighty God, we shall want to base our thinking on a biblical concept of marriage. This study will raise some questions. Is it really the design which is at fault? Or does the failure of so many marriages lie with the husbands and wives who have misinterpreted or ignored God's instructions? Perhaps they have failed in their calling? Maybe they are unwilling to work at a relationship whose success lies more in striving towards the goal of mutual caring than in an initial wave of erotic feeling? Which *is* at fault, marriage or married people?

Opponents of marriage who reject it on the grounds that it constitutes a strait-jacket relationship, that it stultifies the growth of the individual, that it restricts the freedom of man and wife, need to be aware that it is not Christian marriage which they are attacking but sick marriages.

The Bible's picture of marriage, on the other hand, is exciting. It is awesome. It was designed by the Creator Himself (Gn. 2:24). It is regarded as normal (there is no word for 'bachelor' in the Old Testament). It is the basis of society (Gn. 1:26–28), the means of bringing up children 'in the Lord' (Eph. 5:22 – 6:4) and the place where our God-given sexuality may be expressed (1 Cor. 7:1–5). As for the personal relationship of man and wife, marriage is for companionship, helping, completion and togetherness (Gn. 2:18–23; Pr. 5:18–19). It alleviated the aloneness which the first created man felt (Gn. 2:18). The marital relationship is about mutuality and loving (Eph. 5:21ff.). It involves openness, avoids pretence (*cf*. Ps. 51:6) and therefore leads to security and a sense of well-being. There are special promises to couples: the promise of God's presence to those who pray together (Mt. 18:19–20) and the promise that He will unite those who are becoming 'one flesh' (Mk. 10:8–12). Even the command to couples to remain loyal to one another, to leave and to cleave, is not a nutcracker designed to crush your individuality. Rather it is a nutrient which will enable the seeds of your relationship to grow strong, whole and full.

Towards understanding each other

It is my intention to take some of these Bible truths, to use them as a skeleton, and encourage you to add your own flesh and blood to the bones by examining your reactions, expectations and feelings. In this way you prepare yourselves to form a relationship based on Christian principles. It will be a relationship as unique to you as the personalities which you plan to combine. I am not proposing that you embark on a period of introspection. Neither am I encouraging you to indulge in the false honesty that cannot bear to have thoughts and feelings secret from each other. I am suggesting that, from the beginning, you learn to love one another. One important aspect of married love is to learn gradually to unveil your inner thoughts and feelings to one another so that you set out on the journey into marriage better equipped to understand each other. Understanding is an essential ingredient of satisfying relationships, one of the greatest gifts you can give to your partner. But understanding between two strong individuals is not always easily acquired.

It is to help you really to understand each other that I have included certain questions in each chapter. They are printed in italic type. I suggest that you answer them in a particular way. The method may sound strange and, at first, it will feel even more odd than it sounds. All I can say in defence is that many couples, including ourselves, have discovered the value of writing their thoughts and feelings for one another in a notebook kept only for that purpose.

Writing has several advantages over verbal communication. A blank piece of paper never looks bored. It doesn't cry. It is never angry. And it doesn't interrupt your train of thought. Neither does it pay more attention to the more persuasive or vocal partner. The blank page pays equal attention to both points of view. It therefore gives each of you equal opportunity for self-expression.

David and I felt embarrassed when we first started to

9

communicate in this way. We were amazed, therefore, to discover that, through the understanding which grew as we wrote, a new sense of fun and adventure crept into our marriage. For this reason, I have no hesitation in suggesting that you also learn about one another in this fascinating way.

You will each need a fat exercise book. Then, I suggest that you take one chapter of this book at a time and work through the questions which it contains. Set aside half an hour when you can relax together in private and divide the time into three. Spend the first ten minutes responding to the question in the form of a letter to your partner. Then exchange books and, in a leisurely way, applying the rules of good listening (see chapter 3), read through two or three times what your partner has written. The last ten minutes might be extended as you discuss, clarify and pray over what each person has written. When you write, let the emphasis be on self-awareness, 'I feel…'rather than allowing it to become an intellectual exercise, 'I think…'. The word 'feel' has been used in the questions as a reminder. Intellectual discussion has its proper place, of course, but it can easily become an escape route, to avoid facing our real selves.

There is no need for you to wait until the next chapter to make a start. You can begin now with this question:

How do I feel about dedicating myself, my life and my talents to you for the rest of my life?

As you respond to that question and others like it, I believe you will find that in these 'love letters' you have a method of communication for which you will always be thankful. I believe too that, like ours, your excitement about marriage will grow.

Notes for chapter one

1. C. S. Lewis, *A Grief Observed* (Faber, 1961), p.10.
2. Sheldon Vanauken, *A Severe Mercy* (Hodder and Stoughton, 1977), p.43.
3. Fiona Malcolm, 'How to grow in marriage', *Woman's Journal*, Feb. 1980

2 Our Solemn Vow

If you choose to form your union on the basis of God's institution of marriage rather than on the whims of man, or worse, your own fluctuating emotions, these are the sort of questions you will be required to answer:

N. will you take N. to be your wife?

Will you love her, comfort her, honour and protect her, and, forsaking all others, be faithful to her as long as you shall live?

I will.

There are some who argue that the vows are a trap. But a trap is something that ensnares the unsuspecting or holds you against your will. Unlike rabbits whose paws are jammed in the jaws of a gin, you are faced, not with a trap but with a choice. A choice is a decision you make voluntarily in the light of known facts. It is spontaneous. What are the facts? What is it that you propose to promise one another? What is the spirit behind the three major promises: to dedicate your will to the marriage, to love one another and to be faithful?

The dedication of the will

When I was puzzling over the meaning of the promise, 'I will' I thought of my parents. My father was a baker and he met my mother in the bakery where they both worked. They loved to recall the days when they used to kiss and cuddle behind the sacks of flour. My father would cycle seventeen miles each way along dark country lanes so that they could spend a few hours together.

The spring time of their marriage was blighted by the birth, first of a stillborn baby and then of a handicapped child who died. But sorrow united them and in the middle years, the summer of their marriage, they produced three healthy children. Then a further mellowing occurred, a kind of refining of love while my mother's health was failing. Gone now was passion. Each day was an occasion for patience, endurance and kindness as my father nursed his suffering wife. Winter approached. As I stood at my mother's deathbed and watched my father's last, farewell kiss, I realized that his love for her as she lay dying was as powerful as in those fun-filled days when they dodged behind the flour sacks. They had experienced the ebb and flow of marital joy through each season of life and had proved that love is 'strong as death'. On the day of my mother's funeral, my father wrote in his diary, 'The end on earth of a wonderful loving....It was a lovely sunny afternoon.'

On your wedding day you will promise to dedicate your will to one another.

When you dedicate your will to someone for life, you are promising to stand by that person no matter what the future brings. You are no longer open to the option of giving up on marriage. As Christians you believe that it is God's will for your marriage to succeed and, even when terrifying problems appear, it is His grace that is available to see you through. Some of the richest marriages are those that have worked their way through disasters that would have shattered others, but, because they refused to give up and worked towards a solution in partnership *with God*, they reached a maturity and a joy they had never imagined possible.

You are unfettered. You are free to react spontaneously to the questions:

Will you do all in your power to make your marriage succeed?

Are you prepared to dedicate yourself to this partner and to marriage, the most demanding and rewarding of all relationships?

If so, you make a voluntary decision to exercise discipline so that, whenever erotic feelings evaporate, you continue to act lovingly towards one another. Often this is the beginning of the real love which is patient, kind, trusting and always thinks the best (1 Cor. 13:4–7). To act in this way is not hypocrisy; it is working at love with the belief, to borrow John Powell's phrase, that 'love works for those who work at it.'

A promise to love

'How can you promise to love someone for ever?'

The questioner was a young man, puzzled by his rebel emotions. He was engaged to one girl and found himself 'falling in love' with another. His experience was not unlike that of someone who asked me, 'What am I to do? I love my wife but I've 'fallen in love' with an older woman. How can I love two women at once?'

What are you promising when you exchange vows? Are you promising to *feel* romantic love for ever? Clearly marriage vows cannot be based on something as transient as feelings for, as C. S. Lewis puts it, 'no one can promise to go on feeling a certain way. He might as well promise never to have a headache, always to feel hungry.'

Then what are you promising? You are covenanting a love which is more than a feeling. It is maintained by the will. It is about actions. It includes cherishing, sustaining and caring for one another. It is about loyalty and sharing.

When you exchange marriage vows, you are not promising a cheap love, that which costs you nothing. Rather, you are promising to embark on a commitment which will involve you in a costly laying down of yourself, your creativity, your sensitivity and your inventiveness so that the other may grow, you may grow and your marriage may mature.

This growth is one of the delights of marriage. It is one of its purposes. The question love asks is not: 'What shall I get out of marriage?' (though we know that the answer to that is a very positive one) but: 'What can I put into marriage that will bring out the gifts of my partner to our mutual growth?' This is not the same as trying to squeeze your partner into your own mould. It is a matter of helping one another to be the best we can be. God is love, and His institution of marriage is characterized by love-in-action.

This love-in-action has a transforming power. The story of an eccentric Scottish school teacher demonstrates this. He enjoyed great popularity because of the way he reacted to ink blobs. Whenever a child submitted a piece of work, smudged by ink, he would take his own pen and skilfully draw round the blobs transforming them into angels. Such creativity and ingenuity will not turn your partner into an angel but it will draw out much of his/her potential.

Few of us recognize the full potential in our partner when we are newly married. But each of us can coax out that potential through patient loving, gentle persuasion and acts of encouragement. Imaginative loving of this kind enables you to concentrate on your wholeness even in your brokenness. As John Powell points out: 'Who I am, what I become, depends largely on those who love me.'

To promise to love, therefore, is to promise to create a permanent, growing relationship. A recent document explains it well: 'People fall in love; but they do not fall into marriage. Marriage involves the will as well as the emotions. Marriages are *made*. They are "made" in two senses of the word. They are made initially by mutual consent and commitment. They still have to be made through the sharing of life and love.'[1]

This sharing affects the whole of life. Your wedding day is to marriage what the overture is to an opera, the prelude anticipating the forthcoming performance. You must continually move on in your loving, learning to harmonize with one another through all the shades and moods of the drama of your life. This involves a willingness to relish each new thrill, and a willingness also to allow past thrills to die away:

> It is simply no good trying to keep any thrill: this is the very worst thing you can do. Let the thrill go – let it die away – go on through that period of death into the quieter interest and happiness that follow – and you will find you are living in a world of new thrills all the time. But if you…try to prolong them artificially, they will all get weaker and weaker, and fewer and fewer, and you will be a bored, disillusioned old man for the rest of your life.[2]

But disillusionment does not erode a marriage built, not only on the thrill of romantic love, but on the love which goes beyond feelings, which is kind, believes all things and means that you are simply there, on the same side as the other. Paul Simon expresses this idea well:

> If you need a friend....
> Like a bridge over troubled water I will lay me down.

It is expressed rather differently by George Eliot:

> Oh! the comfort, the inexpressible comfort of feeling safe with a person, having neither to weigh thoughts nor measure words but pour them all right out just as they are, chaff and grain together, knowing that a faithful hand will take and sift them, keep what is worth keeping and then with the breath of kindness blow the rest away.

How do you know whether you love each other enough to exchange vows? Erotic love blurs the reality of a relationship in the same way as a heat haze distorts the landscape. Respond to this suggestion in your notebook:

When romantic feelings are not strong what I like about you is...

Then consider three further questions:

Do I believe in you sufficiently to want to stay alongside you through all the moods and changes of life?

In what ways do we enjoy expressing the love Paul describes in 1 Corinthians 13?

What latent abilities and characteristics do I detect in you? How might I seek to draw these out?

Promising faithfulness

God, the bridegroom of Israel, exemplifies the true meaning of faithfulness in marriage. God remains a 'resource person' for His bride no matter what mood she chooses. He woos His wayward bride (Ho. 14), gently chastens His sinful bride (Is. 59:1–2) and readily forgives His returning bride (Is. 55:7). God's faithfulness *appears* to have wavered in times of frustration (Is. 54:7–8) but it never failed.

Thus the Bible helps us to understand that faithfulness is not primarily negative, 'I will never leave you', 'I won't look at other men'. Rather, faithfulness has an assertive ring. It is a strong quality which contributes to the up-building of the marriage relationship.

Faithfulness is a voluntary donation, a free investment of one-self in the partnership. It is a promise to share your possessions, a mutual offering of body, mind and spirit for the enrichment of both partners and the relationship. As such, a marriage built on fidelity holds out the promise and expectation of a new life for both individuals.

Faithfulness also implies that each partner has worth, that each has something to give the other, that each will find completion in the other. Faithfulness does not mean that you two will be the only 'resource people' for one another; it does mean that you will seek completion first in the other. Henri Nouwen warns that it is possible for married partners to have false Messianic expectations of one another:

> No friend or lover, no husband or wife, no community or commune will be able to put at rest our deepest craving for unity and wholeness. And by burdening others with these divine expectations, of which we ourselves are often only partially aware, we might inhibit the expression of free friendship and love and evoke instead feelings of in adequacy and weakness. Friendship and love.....ask for gentle fearless space in which we can move to and from each other.[3]

Fidelity means that married people promise to support one another while recognizing their inevitable limitations. An understanding of God's love assures them that there is a deeper refuge to be found in the One who is love, God Himself.

The value of this 'other-wordly' love, the divine, is a vital clue to the search for the ability to deny oneself, to live unselfishly and act sacrificially. This self-investment required by faithfulness necessitates a certain renunciation of what has gone before. The dependence of childhood must be left behind, you must abdicate certain bachelor or spinster freedoms and you must abandon a life-style which was consistent only with the single state. If you are to form a life long union of fidelity with your partner you must be prepared to bid a fond farewell to 'number one'.

But men, in particular, seem to find this aspect of faithfulness irksome. Fiona Malcolm exposes the pretence of some of

them: 'Walk into any pub at six-thirty in the evening and you
will see this: queues of husbands line up to use the public
phone: "Hello, darling. Listen, you won't believe this, but
it's been another of those days. The client's still with me..."'[4]

Women also have difficulties with faithfulness. The film
Kramer versus Kramer, in which a young wife and mother
leaves home, abandoning her husband and small child,
illustrates that women, too, are unprepared for the sacrifices
involved in the vow of fidelity. Some women will choose to
leave home as soon as faithfulness makes inroads on their
'need' to succeed in life.

And Christians are not exempt from this malaise. Most
live churches offer a plethora of meetings which could involve
one or both or you most nights of the week. Christian activities,
however worthwhile, must not be allowed to bite off a dis-
proportionate chunk of your time. They must not become an
escape from the hard work essential to creating a good relationship with your partner. I am not suggesting that as newly-
weds you should withdraw from all activities. I am suggesting
that you nurture your marriage, that you recognize that your
marriage is more important than your work, your hobbies or
even attendance at church meetings. Fidelity is a time-
consuming vocation, requiring energy and concentration.

Two persons promising to dedicate their will, their powers
of loving and their fidelity to one partnership in the duration
of a lifetime create a relationship as fascinating and with as
many permutations as a kaleidoscope. It has been described
in this way:

We use the term 'marriage' to describe a cluster of expectations about the relationship of a man and a woman. We
expect it to be a loving relationship, based on mutual
attraction and shared values; a sexual relationship, based
on physical attraction and shared physical satisfaction; a
biological relationship, leading to the birth and nurture of
children; a social relationship, involving the family of
marriage in a network of wider family and community
contacts; an economic relationship, based on a common
domicile, the marital home, and a sharing of possessions
and income...We expect this complex web of relationships

to be exclusive, and to last throughout the joint lives of the partners.'[5]

Marriage leads to a rich and varied relationship. But it would be surprising if you never felt precarious or disappointed with your partnership. The probability is that you will fail to detect the beauty of the patterns in the kaleidoscope as they are created. But in asking the following questions of one another from time to time you will be able to trace some of the designs emerging from your particular union:

What do I have to invest in our marriage at the moment?

What are we doing to draw on the resources offered us by God?

Does our order of priorities seem right at the moment?

Am I withholding time, energy, concentration or practical love from our relationship unnecessarily? Why?

If you intersperse months of patient, happy 'jogging along' with occasions when you answer penetrating questions like those, you will discover that you are writing a personal journal of marriage. The story, as it unfolds, will contain both exciting moments and unnerving ones. But it will be a story of growth and developing satisfaction.

Notes for chapter two

1. *Marriage and the Church's Task* (Church Information Office, 1978), p.34.
2. C. S. Lewis, *Mere Christianity* (Geoffrey Bles, 1952), p.87.
3. Henri Nouwen, *Reaching out* (Fount, 1976), p.31.
4. Fiona Malcolm, 'How to grow in marriage', *Woman's Journal*, Feb. 1980.
5. *Marriage and the Church's Task,* p.16.

3 Listening and Communicating

The Genesis story makes it clear that, in the early days, Adam did not have a soul-friend. In the absence of another human being who understood him, he seems to have experienced an emptiness which caused God to observe that 'it is not good for man to be alone.' God's remedy for this aloneness was to bring to him another person. And 'Adam knew Eve'.

The Hebrew word 'to know' includes sexual intimacy, intellectual oneness and emotional understanding. From the outset it would appear that the Bible model for marriage embraced a three-dimensional intimacy, of body, mind and spirit. Every human being needs the assurance that he is accepted, understood and heard. When a person feels 'known', understood, he experiences love, his assurance of self-worth increases and he is contented. This assurance can come whether you are married or not, supremely through God's own presence but also through the fellowship of other believers. Nor is the need for being understood, of course, by any means the only reason for marrying, but it follows that when the person who so seeks to understand you is your life-partner, you become alive to him/her in such a way that trust, enjoyment and adventure characterize your relationship to a special degree.

Most couples today sail into marriage assuming that they do know one another, most are anxious to communicate and eager to listen to the other, but each partner is capable of blocking real encounter with a barricade of fear.

There is the fear of hurting the other and the fear that your partner might hurt you. Maybe if you are really open with one another old wounds will smart again or past bruises be hurt. There is the fear that your spouse might judge you, criticize you or blame you for shortcomings which, so far, you know you have failed to conquer or correct. There is the fear of not being heard accurately, or being misunderstood, and worse, of being rejected by the person closest to you. There is the fear of becoming a burden, imposing, or casting a shadow over your partner's happiness. If your self-esteem is low, the most crippling fear of all often goes unexpressed. It is the fear that if you expose yourself as you really are, your partner may not love you any more.

You can do either of two things with these fears. You can play a game of 'let's pretend' and deny their existence with the vain hope that ignoring fears will drive them away. Or you can acknowledge them, and take the risk of expressing them to your partner.

Playing 'let's pretend'

Doreen experimented with both methods shortly after her marriage to Barry and quickly discovered that playing 'let's pretend' created a tangle in the lines of communication which resulted in pain and confusion for herself and her husband.

When she married Barry, Doreen had sparkle. She was fun-loving and he enjoyed being with her. Within two months of their wedding day all that had changed. She lacked energy, she cried a great deal and became withdrawn. Barry could not understand the gradual change in her but nursed secret feelings of guilt and fear, suspecting that he was failing her in some way.

Doreen gave him no clue. They would go off to work each morning as usual. They used to share the preparation of the evening meal and the washing-up before going out together or just relaxing in the home they were so proud of. They would make love frequently, a part of being married they'd looked forward to, for both were demonstrative people. Doreen used to say that everything was fine, but the absence of her usual bright smile exposed the words as mere pretence.

Doreen couldn't bring herself to tell Barry what was wrong. Eventually, she came to me for help. She sobbed as she told me that she had failed to reach a climax when they were making love. She felt cheated of her rights. She was afraid to tell Barry. After all she didn't want to spoil his happiness or drive a wedge between them.

Since playing 'let's pretend' had clearly failed, I suggested the four of us should meet to confront both the fears and the facts. When David and I met Barry and Doreen together they both poured out the pent-up feelings obstructing their understanding of one another. Doreen's fears of hurting Barry proved groundless. Barry was relieved to hear the truth. He assured Doreen that he still loved and wanted her.

This young couple need not have suffered so much if they had observed some of the 'rules' of good commuication. Frank talking and accurate listening could have helped both of them.

Some 'rules' for good communication

Everyone uses a variety of 'languages', verbal and non-verbal. It sometimes happens that a person will give you one message verbally while communicating an entirely different impression with their eyes, posture, facial expression, hands or tone of voice. Doreen, for example, insisted that everything was fine, although her eyes were sad and her face wore only a 'plastic' smile. She was giving Barry a 'mixed message' which confused him because it confronted him with a series of choices; to listen to her verbal reassurance and reject the non-verbal message, to attend to the non-verbal language and ignore her words, or to reject both. It would have helped him to know that usually the non-verbal message is the more accurate of the two.

The Psalmist reminds us that the Lord requires 'truth in the inward parts' (Ps. 51:6 AV). That means, among other things, keeping our integrity by communicating as honestly and accurately as possible with our words and our body. Barry could have checked out with Doreen exactly what she was trying to say. If he had gently asked, 'I seem to hear you *saying* everything is all right, but I feel you aren't as bright as usual. Am I making a mistake?' he might have saved the situation. In clarifying like this it is important not to appear to judge: 'you're lying', or to condemn: 'you ought to be happy with such a lovely home', or even to blame: 'you're saying one thing and acting another and you're making me confused.' Moreover, it is vital that you bear responsibility for the way you are interpreting the situation, 'I feel...' not, 'you are...' If your partner feels 'put down' by you, or if you start to score points off one another, you strangle the attempt to talk intimately.

Barry fell into a trap. He read the signs, misinterpreted them and made assumptions which confirmed his worst fears. 'I'm failing her. She doesn't want me. I'll withdraw from her.'

The couple could have been thrown into even greater confusion if Doreen had chosen to play two other games: dropping hints or expecting Barry to become a mind-reader. She didn't expect Barry to 'just know', though many partners do make this unrealistic demand of one another. The painful truth is this: if you want your partner to understand how you feel, you must be willing to spell it out.

Doreen found it costly to share her innermost feelings with Barry, but it was a risk worth taking. They both learned that night that when you begin to share deeply with another, you feel vulnerable and you need the assurance that your partner is listening with attention, patience and care.

As Paul Tournier puts it: 'It is impossible to over-emphasize the immense need we have to be really listened to, to be taken seriously, to be understood...No one can develop freely in this world and find full life without feeling understood by at least one person.'[1] I believe that when the person who cares enough about you to listen to you is your partner in marriage, three things happen: the whole relationship functions on a deeper, stronger level, as partners you are drawn into a oneness which cannot easily be broken and you suffuse your relationship with the kind of warmth that brings security.

Learning to listen

If you want to listen well, one form of demonstrating love to your partner, you will attempt to see the world through the other's eyes without either becoming sucked into the bog of his/her negative emotions or being unduly persuaded or caught up in the other's positive feelings.

We have already seen that it is possible to learn as much from someone by listening to their non-verbal messages as by hearing their words. Eyes, for example, speak a language. They mirror bottled-up emotions. For this reason a person will sometimes avoid the gaze of another. They would feel too exposed if someone else saw the fear, the sorrow or the pain reflected in their eyes.

Posture is also a language. Drooping shoulders are usually a sign of weary spirits, while a person who walks with spring and purpose is probably enjoying life.

The tone of a person's voice is another measure of his/her emotions. A dull, monotonous, flat voice often expresses the dreariness of spirit which the person is experiencing. A whining voice, on the other hand, might indicate a subtle plan to manipulate, while a high-pitched voice which speaks quickly, could tell you that the person is excited or distressed.

People communicate tension in a variety of ways. Clenched fists and restless hands tell you a great deal about a person. And facial expression: the smile, the frown, the blank look, 'empty', far-away eyes, speak a language which might never be translated into words.

Tears are also a language. They are sometimes an expression of anger, bitterness or fear. Sometimes they are the overflow of sorrow, sadness or grief. And sometimes people weep tears of joy. It is important, therefore, if you are uncertain why your partner is crying, to ask, with gentleness, 'What are these tears trying to say?'

When you listen, you too are communicating. If you listen attentively to your partner, you give the assurance that you feel your partner is of worth, that he/she is of such value to you that you are prepared to give time and attention. But you can as easily give non-verbal signals which convey non-acceptance. If you listen to another with one anxious eye on the clock, or if you drum your fingers on the arm of the chair, yawn or leap to the telephone as soon as it rings, then your partner will feel that you are bored, and real communication will stop.

As you listen, you can by-pass words with the silent language of touch. A comforting arm around the shoulder, a gentle touch, an outstretched hand, convey all the under-standing, love and cherishing which is required on some occasions.

What I have just written may sound obvious. The facts before us are so obvious that many of us fail to appropriate them. But I want to underline their importance because sensitive communicating and good listening are essential to healthy relationships.

As Christians you start with an advantage. You will have already opened yourselves to allow the growth of the fruit of the Spirit in your lives: joy, peace, patience, kindness, good-ness, long-suffering, gentleness, self-control and the non-judgmental love which always thinks the best. When two people apply these characteristics to the hard work of listening and communicating, they will grow in understanding.

But to listen with sensitivity to the person closest to you is not easy. It is difficult for a variety of reasons.

Difficulties in communication

Most couples find that there are times when to listen to one another is impossible. When our own feelings of joy, frus-tration, tiredness or pain are strong, most of us do not even want to listen to anyone else. All available energy has been used up in listening to our own feelings.

One wife expressed it well when she wrote to me recently. She had been suffering from sleeplessness, was over-eating and anxious about her work. Her husband, she felt, took little interest in her, and feelings of rejection gnawed away inside her. She was so taken up with her own problems that she had no energy to listen to her husband's need for support while he started a new job. Even when he arrived home with a black eye one day, she failed to notice! Her husband, on the other hand, was so excited about his future prospects that he couldn't be bothered to listen to his wife's anxieties. He deliberately ignored the signals which she gave him. They distanced one another and set in motion a cold war of silence until eventually the pent-up emotions blew up and they had a row.

A pale reflection of that extreme example occurs in most homes on many occasions. Tension is caused when a husband

24

arrives home after a frustrating day to discover that his wife is also feeling miserable. His own exasperation blinds him to the signs that his wife has had a disappointing day too. She fails to notice how tired and dejected he looks. She assumes that he is annoyed with her. And so the scene is set for another domestic flare-up. It will probably erupt over something trivial or maybe the couple will keep a safe distance from one another.

They will keep conversation on a superficial level, and superficiality is a hindrance to good communication. Most people answer the question, 'How are you?' with the expected answer, 'I'm fine', even if they are on the way to hospital. We have been trained in the art of deceit. 'How nice you look today', can cover a variety of unexpressed opinions. And many of us are adept at handing out empty invitations like, 'Do come and see me sometime.' We know that invitations like that are safe because 'sometime' is usually no time.

We should not be suprised, therefore, when, stripped of the jargon we have learned and the masks we normally wear, we find it hard to share our real feelings with another. But, as John Powell writes, 'My emotions are the key to me. When I give you this key, you can come into me, and share with me the most precious gift I have to offer you, "myself".'[2]

How do I feel about communicating and listening?

What are my feelings about sharing my inner thoughts, attitudes and emotions with you?

Notes for chapter three

1. Paul Tournier, *Marriage Difficulties* (SCM Press, 1967), p.29.
2. John Powell, *The Secret of Staying in Love* (Argus, 1974), p.78.

4 Degrees of Involvement

The high incidence of marital breakdown in Britain and other parts of the western world has reached crisis proportions. Marriage counsellors, the clergy and sociologists, alarmed by the statistics before them, have been examining possible reasons why couples fail to create satisfying marriages.

Some blame marriage as an institution, claiming that to invite two people to share every aspect of their lives for fifty years or more is to set in motion a claustrophobic relationship which makes unreasonable demands. Others are claiming that traditional marriages, where the husband was the bread winner and the wife the home-maker, failed because there was insufficient intimacy. Couples, it is claimed, were held together in a cold, unbreakable bondage of respectability, not by the more desirable ties of warmth, togetherness and trust.

Loud voices are demanding that traditional marriages should be discarded as something dog-eared and outgrown. The emphasis in the proposed new-style marriage is on freedom. Yet none of the alternative proposals are suitable substitutes for the couple who desire to submit their relationship to God and His plans for marriage. The onus lies, then, on each couple to work out for themselves the answer to the question, 'what do *I* expect from marriage?'

This is a crucial question. The experts are agreed that one of the chief reasons why marriages are failing today is that couples are not encouraged to examine their hopes for their relationship before they commit themselves to it. The need to look ahead is no new discovery, of course. Jesus Himself said,

'Which of you, desiring to build a tower, does not first sit down and count the cost, whether he has enough to complete it?' (Lk. 14:28). If you have never stopped to examine your expectations of the marriage relationship, you won't know whether you have fulfilled them. But, like many couples before you, you may be left with a hollow sense of disillusionment.

No-one is suggesting that couples should expect to plot aims and goals for the whole of their life together. That would be foolish because hopes and desires clarify and change with the years. But couples are being urged to examine their hopes for the early years of marriage.

Social custom places enormous emphasis on 'the wedding' and very little on the ensuing marriage. But the wedding day is not the finishing tape. It is the starting line. And you need to plan beyond the day itself. *What do I expect from our marriage?* Your response to that question will help you to discover particular areas where you need to work hard at your relationship. It will show you what you hope to achieve. It will clarify your personal aims and help you to set realistic ones.

If you are already married, of course, it is still not too late to work at that question. In some ways you may be in a better position to do so than the engaged couple. It is a question which all couples need to ask at various stages of their marriage.

In suggesting some possible ways of approaching this key question, I propose to base our thinking, not on traditional marriage, nor on the alternative patterns being offered today, but on one of the purposes for marriage which I find in the Bible. It may be summed up in the word, 'involvement'.

'Involvement' in the Bible

We have already seen that Adam and Eve, in knowing one another, were involved with each other sexually, emotionally and intellectually. The Bible frequently speaks of marriage as a close relationship. This closeness is reflected in the Old Testament where God is described as the bridegroom of Israel. This imagery both illustrates and is illustrative of human marriage. In this role of bridegroom God becomes thoroughly involved with His wayward bride. He pours out tenderness, care and material provision upon her. Ezekiel describes the Lord's child bride whom He discovers and cherishes through each phase of her life and dearly loves her, (Ezk. 16:6–10). In another place, God expresses unending love for His bride: 'With everlasting love I have taken pity on you...the mountains may depart, the hills be shaken, but my love for you will never leave you' (Is. 54:8,10 JB). His physical and emotional provision for her outstrips her periods of disloyalty, coolness and adultery and His ready acceptance and approval of Israel draws forth all her potential beauty, here seen as masculine, 'I will love them with all my heart...I will fall like dew on Israel. He shall bloom like the lily...he will have the beauty of the olive and the fragrance of Lebanon' (Ho. 14:5–6 JB).

This symbolism is developed in the New Testament which describes the church as the bride of Christ. The incarnation is about intimate involvement. The crucifixion is about painful identification. The message of the ascending Christ is that He departs in order to prepare a place where His bride might join Him, where she might be involved with Him for ever. Paul also uses this imagery as a basis for teaching the early Christians in Corinth (1 Cor. 7), Ephesus (Eph. 5) and Colossae (Col. 3) about marriage.

The Bible's expectation of marriage implies involvement in the life and thought of the partner; friendship and companionship. God and His bride do not appear to have lived parallel lives with little reference to one another. On the contrary the Bible uses warm words to describe the relationship: tenderness, care, unending love. It also uses demanding words: self-giving, sacrifice and hard work. Clearly, the purpose of marriage is that each partner should love the other (Eph. 5:25; Tit. 2:4). The effects of mutual loving of the kind the Bible describes will be, among others, a growing sense of security, well-being and togetherness.

Do we then enter marriage purely to gratify our own sense of need or wanting to be loved? If we do we may be heading for disaster. We may, in fact, be acting very selfishly. Married love is about giving, and it may hurt. The deep intimacy of which the Bible speaks is the result of costly

28

self-giving love of the kind Christ demonstrated.

And the Bible does not hide the fact that the work of achieving true togetherness and becoming involved with one's life-partner is the toil of a lifetime, which creates disappointment as well as joy. If even the bride of God is described as an 'unhappy creature, storm-tossed, disconsolate' (Is. 54:11 JB), because of her failure to maintain a covenant relationship, married couples do well to anticipate similar, albeit transient phases of unhappiness. Hosea describes God's agonizing work in wooing His adulterous bride back to Himself: 'Ephraim, how could I part with you? Israel, how could I give you up?...My heart recoils from it, my whole being trembles at the thought' (Ho. 11:8 JB). The New Testament reminds us that Christ stripped Himself of glory, descended to the depths of horror and shame, to woo back the bride who was so far away from Him. The Bible does not promise an easy ride. It does present intimacy as a goal towards which we travel and marriage as a gift packed with the delights of love.

The Bible pattern for marriage, then, models self-giving love, in imitation of God's involvement. It nowhere suggests total fusion, where one partner loses his/her identity in the other. The task before you is to decide how you will give expression to mutual involvement in a way which is applicable to your relationship and consistent with your aims. This will vary from couple to couple as David and Vera Mace have shown.

Maximum, limited or minimum

The Maces devised a diagrammatic model suggesting three possible alternatives facing married couples: marriage of maximum involvement, in which you each retain your individuality while your lives overlap to a considerable extent, marriage of minimum involvement where the small degree of overlap with one another still constitutes a union but opportunities for individual freedom are greater, and marriage of limited involvement which lies somewhere between the two. In diagrammatic form the three options look like this:

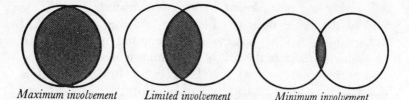

Maximum involvement   *Limited involvement*   *Minimum involvement*

The advantages of a marriage of minimum involvement attract many couples today. Infrequent interaction makes the likelihood of disagreement and quarrels unlikely. The occasional flare-ups seem insignificant when balanced with the variety of life's experiences, but the relationship provides each partner with a modicum of togetherness and makes few demands.

Karen and Steve were relieved to opt for this pattern of marriage. They both came from broken homes, both suffered from a lack of self-worth, so felt that marriageability prospects were limited. But both felt love-starved enough to reach out for the consolation they believed marriage offered. They knew that, for them, to marry was to take a great risk. Their story to date is a happy one.

Now they are married they each retain a high degree of individuality by working full-time and pursuing time-consuming hobbies separate from one another. They eat together each evening, enjoy sexual intercourse of a perfunctory nature three or four times each week, and sometimes, though not always, go on holiday together. In this way, Karen and Steve have found more happiness in marriage than either dared to hope for because they were brave enough to set realistic goals for their union.

David and I, on the other hand, expected to move from engagement to a marriage of maximum involvement in one neat step. Neither of us expressed our hopes and neither of us squealed when, like two hedgehogs, we snuggled into one another, stabbing each other with the indefinable prickles which formed a part of both of us. We suffered the shock silently and recoiled a little from one another before plucking up the unexpressed courage to start again. We didn't know then what we understand more clearly now, that maximum involvement with another person, allowing one's life to overlap significantly, even with one you love, is costly. It can feel like deprivation of privacy. It requires a high level of maturity from each person.

Psychiatrist Jack Dominian describes what this maturity involves. He claims that both partners must have achieved emotional independence, absolute trust in one another and complete self-acceptance. Moreover, he suggests that, not only must they be able to give themselves to one another without reserve but they must both possess the willingness to receive love from the other. Maximum involvement necessitates persons in whom anxiety, aggression and jealousy have ceased to dwell. It requires couples who consistently offer one another kindness, patience and gentleness; who are long-suffering and who exercise self-control (1 Cor. 13:4–7).

On looking back, we now realize that for us maximum involvement was an unattainable goal.

We now know that no couple succeeds in every area of their relationship immediately and so we keep the goal of maximum involvement before us still. It remains our cherished dream.

Some couples, realizing that maximum involvement is unrealistic or, for them, undesirable, even threatening, settle for the goal of limited involvement which grants to both ample space for individualism while including an overlap of interest and activities.

What kind of marriage do you want? Are you aiming for a marriage of maximum involvement, minimum involvement or limited involvement? Why?

What kind of marital relationship is it reasonable for you two to expect in the light of what has been said about emotional maturity, trust and self-acceptance?

In what areas will your lives overlap comfortably? Where might involvement cause discomfort to one or both of you? How do you plan to cope with your differences?

Are you willing to make the necessary sacrifices to ensure that your relationship grows in depth, warmth and trust?

Are you willing to lay aside those hopes which, for you, are unrealistic and unattainable?

Most couples go into marriage with unrealistic expectations

of one another. When the high hopes of their relationship are not realized, the fear that perhaps they are incompatible creeps in. They are not necessarily assessing the marriage accurately. Often, disappointment can goad them into learning to complete and complement one another.

As you work at your relationship, particularly in the early days of marriage, it is worth remembering that, although few admit it, most married couples hunger for more intimacy than they have found. They therefore swing between maximum and limited involvement. Neither is 'right' or wrong', 'better' or 'best'. They fulfil different needs at different times. The average couple achieves closeness only in a limited area of their relationship and for a short period of time. Nurturing relationships requires hours of patient drawing together. It does not just happen.

5 Two Becoming One

What are your feelings about becoming one?

A middle-aged editor was invited to compare his relationship with his wife, whom he had divorced, with his friendship with Maria, a woman with whom he was living outside of marriage. He replied, 'My relationship with Maria is solider and tighter than my marriage ever was. Why? Because every morning when I wake up and look at her lying there next to me, I know she totally wants to be there, not because of some ink on a piece of paper. This time I won't let that document get between me and a good relationship.'[1]

Acid remarks about the institution of marriage are not new. As we have seen there is a clamour to change the laws concerning marriage. There is the claim that life-long monogamy is good for the church and useful for the tax-collector but it is harmful for the individual: 'like snakes, we need occasionally to shed our old skins and often we cannot do that if we are tied by bonds of guilt to an outgrown love.'[2] Serial monogamy, by which it is customary for a person to be married two or three times during his life, and in which different partners will meet different needs at various phases, is suggested by some.

George and Nena O'Neill offer 'open marriage', their design to replace the old marriage contract which, they believe, '*is* unrealistic and its archaic clauses demand unreasonable commitments.'[3] Partners in an 'open marriage' relationship would re-write their own contract from time to time and each revision would aim to maintain intimacy within the partnership while removing all obstacles to 'freedom'.

Restrictions of any kind are taboo. Anything is allowable, including sexual relations outside the marriage, which, it is claimed, can enrich all partnerships.

Many young people, suffering from the effects of their parents' bitter marital experiences, choose to experiment with group marriages, to live in communes or simply to form non-contractual relationships with a lover rather than allow themselves to be drawn into the 'trap' of marriage.

Popular opinion may mock and the sick marriages of society may appear to substantiate the claims that marriage is outmoded, but that does not alter the admonition of Jesus that 'A man shall leave his father and mother and be joined to his wife, and the two shall become one flesh' (Mk. 10:7–8). He does not start with man, nor with anthropology, but with God: 'from the beginning of creation, "God made them male and female"' (Mk. 10:6). I am not suggesting that we disregard all the opinions of sociologists. I believe they have valuable insights to share. I am saying that, as Christians, we take our authority from God and we need to re-examine the instructions of our Lord, to leave, cleave (be joined) and become one flesh. Our Creator always wants what is best for us and His instructions for marriage are exactly fitted to men and women as they really are. Some of what follows will be painful to read and even more painful to act upon. But the rewards are thrilling.

'Leaving'

If you marry in an Anglican church, traditional in style, you may dramatize the act of 'leaving' during the wedding service. I think of John and Mary's wedding which took place in an ancient church in Yorkshire. Mary walked down the aisle, clutching her father's arm. In that small village she was well known and the church was full of relatives, friends and acquaintances, but it was Mary's father who represented us in 'giving her away'. When they reached the steps at the front of the church, he placed Mary's hand into the vicar's, enacting our willingness that she should be given to John. As soon as John and Mary had exchanged vows, they joined hands and deliberately walked away from the congregation. Alone and apart they moved into the sanctuary. They were leaving relatives and friends so that they could begin the work of cleaving to one another.

'Leaving' is a deliberate act. It is a painful act. If often produces problems, but it is an essential task for married couples. It finds its parallel in childbirth. When a baby is born, the midwife cuts the umbilical cord. The baby has reached the end of one phase of life and begun another. Newly-weds, similarly, must learn to leave behind former means of support and attempt to become primary 'resource persons' for one another. Leaving does not mean they must have no relationships outside their partnership. It does mean that there is no room for entanglements.

Herein lies a problem for couples whose doting parents have learned to live through their children and who find it hard to let go. We return to this problem in chapter 13.

This was the experience of Dave and Di. Di was from a broken home. Both her parents were lonely, isolated people. She felt a keen responsibility for both of them. Before she was married she would spend a lot of time with each of them. She saw this as her Christian duty as well as a way of expressing the love she felt for them. When she married Dave she moved miles from her parents. She wanted the freedom to develop her relationship with Dave but felt guilty about the hurt this caused her mum and dad. It took months for this couple to work through the frustration in a satisfactory way, but eventually they felt sufficiently 'at one' to face the situation together. This happened when Di recognized that, whatever her parents' feelings and needs, her first responsibility was to Dave, and when Dave was able to assure her that there were now two of them to care for her parents.

Dave and Di were glad that they learned to cleave so that they could offer joint love to Di's parents.

This family felt the inevitable pain of leaving. Parents feel the sadness of separation. The couple also feel sad at leaving behind people who have contributed so much to their past. Friends too experience pain. It is unnerving when you don't know whether your friend will want to revive the companionship you have enjoyed so far. The presence of pain does not

35

make leaving wrong. It does make it costly. A kind of 'dying' is part of 'leaving'. This is not death caused by decay. Rather it is the kind of dying which heralds the new life of togetherness. 'Leaving' is for 'cleaving'.

'Cleaving'

'I hate the thought of being glued to another person in marriage.' The speaker was a student asking my advice about her engagement. She really believed that 'to cleave' implied a rigid relationship in which she as the woman would be stuck for ever to her husband. Others have an even more frightening concept. They fear that just as bindweed entwines itself around a thriving plant, strangling it, so married couples end up by stifling one another. But the word 'cleave' as it is used in the Bible does not mean rigidity nor strangulation. It does imply warm togetherness and support. The word is used in the book of Ruth. We read that Ruth 'clave' to Naomi when they were suffering from bereavement (Ru. 1:14 AV). In cleaving to one another they were rescued from the isolation and pain of aloneness. At the end of the book we read of Naomi's joy at the birth of a son to Boaz and Ruth.

Cleaving here implies togetherness in joy and companionship in times of change. The word 'cleave' is used again in 2 Samuel (2:20) to describe the men of Judah who offered loyal support to their king when he least expected it. Loyalty is one of the ingredients of cleaving. It means that your support of one another will transcend criticism. When others criticize your partner, you will not break your trust. Even when *you* feel disappointed in the other, you will continue to believe in him/her. Love 'believes all things' (1 Cor. 13:7).

One flesh

Jesus' teaching about the 'one flesh' relationship contains a promise: 'the two *shall become* one flesh' (Mk. 10:8). Claiming God's promise for your marriage is not only a profound experience but it adds spice to it. It is humbling to think of Almighty God making firm your partnership.

This same verse in Mark's Gospel suggests that becoming one flesh is a gradual process. Becoming one with another is a quiet, imperceptible 'happening' like the unseen intertwining of the roots of two plants growing in the same window-box.

This intertwining is not the same as total fusion. It is a combination of fusion and union. If you fuse two people together, one, or both, lose their identity. They are in danger of submerging their individuality. The relationship could stifle growth. A true 'one-flesh' relationship includes both togetherness and space. As Kahlil Gibran advises:

> together you shall be for evermore. You shall be together when the white wings of death scatter your days...But let there be spaces in your togetherness. And let the winds of the heavens dance between you...Sing and dance together and by joyous, but let each one of you be alone, even as the strings of a lute are alone though they quiver to the same music.[4]

Maria Rilke goes further, suggesting that 'a good marriage is that in which each appoints the other guardian of his solitude.'

How do you feel when your partner wants to be alone, to have space and privacy?

Becoming 'one flesh' has sexual connotations. When two bodies unite to become one, they express the love-commitment they have made and they deepen that commitment. It is a cycle. Two people unite sexually in order to express love and in giving love sexual expression, they nurture it so that it grows.

'One flesh' does not primarily refer to sexual intimacy, however. It is a reference to the closest possible relationship one person can develop with another. Just as Adam referred to Eve as one of his own kind (Gn. 2:23 GNB), his 'kinsman', so in the total self-giving of the one-flesh relationship, husband and wife form a new unit. They become kinsmen, the basis of a new family. But this does not mean that they remain frozen together. As David and Vera Mace put it: 'More accurately (marriage) is the intricate and graceful co-operation of two dancers who through long practice have learned to match each other's movements and moods in response to the music of the spheres.'[5]

Christians believe that this co-operation lasts for ever. It is permanent. As Jesus said, 'What therefore God has joined together, let not man put asunder' (Mk. 10:9). It is here, at this point of permanence, that we part company with the O'Neills and others who claim that such demands are unreasonable and archaic. In advocating permanence, Jesus is not the divine spoil-sport depriving human beings of their fun. The stern admonition to permanence contains a safeguard. God knew that men and women could form an in-depth partnership of the kind we have outlined only within the security of a lifelong commitment.

Psychiatrists researching into the high incidence of marital breakdown seem to be saying something similar. They record the correlation between physical and psychological illness and the insecurity people suffer when their marriage threatens to disintegrate. If they are right in deducing that sleeplessness, nausea, suicidal feelings and depression, to mention a few symptoms, relate to insecurity, and that insecurity is a powerful factor contributing to marriage breakdown, their research underlines Jesus' standard for marriage.

As you consider your future, it is your responsibility to investigate some far-reaching questions:

How do you feel about the marriage ceremony and the marriage certificate?

Do you feel they might bind you together in a bondage of guilt?

What do you feel about the permanence of the relationship you are creating?

Do you think that to require permanence is unreasonable, or do you agree with Bonhoeffer's wedding sermon for his niece in which he said:

As the crown makes the king, and not just his determination to rule, so marriage and not just your love for each other makes you husband and wife in the sight of God and man…As God is infinitely higher than man, so the sanctity, the privilege and the promise of marriage are higher than the sanctity, the privilege and the promise of love. It is not your love which sustains the marriage, but from now on the marriage that sustains your love.[6]

Bonhoeffer's sermon reminds me of the cedar tree in my in-laws' garden. Its vast girth stands firmly rooted, unmoved, sustaining the twin trunks which emerge higher up. That tree speaks to me of a good marriage; of security, freedom and usefulness; it symbolizes two separates united, yet apart; magnificent yet still growing. It is a constant reminder of *God's* plan for marriage.

Notes for chapter five

1. Quoted by Nena and George O'Neill, *Open Marriage* (Abacus, 1973), pp.15-16.
2. Fiona Malcolm, 'How to grow in marriage', *Woman's Journal*, Feb. 1980.
3. Nena and George O'Neill, *op.cit.*, p.19.
4. Kahlil Gibran, *The Prophet* (Heinemann, 1926), p.16.
5. David and Vera Mace, *We can have better marriages if we want them* (Oliphants, no date), p.5.
6. Dietrich Bonhoeffer, *Letters and Papers from Prison* (Fontana, 1959), p.150.

6 Love and Submission

'Few contemporary women in the west today marry with the notion of obeying or submitting to their husbands.' On the contrary, 'the principle of equality is being emphasised.'[1]

Does the submission question worry you? Why? Does it emerge in practice in your relationship? Often? Do you think it should?

'Joyce, are you a submissive wife?' The question came from Lee Ling, an attractive Chinese friend, and it took me by surprise. It left me feeling threatened. I could offer no easy answer to the string of questions which followed. 'What does it mean to be a submissive wife, to obey one's husband? Does the headship of the husband mean that women are inferior to men, that husbands have the right to boss their wives around? Lee Ling's cultural background and the Christian teaching she had received suggested to her that the answer to the last two questions was 'yes'. But like many young wives today she found herself rebelling at the thought of being her husband's slave.

Like Lee Ling I had trained for a profession before I became a wife. I found motherhood gave me great joy and fulfilment but it did not cancel out my enjoyment of teaching. Many aspects of home-making are a delight for me but I have never lost my love of speaking, writing and counselling. Ten years ago I was struggling to hold in tension the pull towards personal fulfilment, which I suspected a return to my profession would give me, and what I then understood 'submission' to mean.

In those days it was fashionable in the Christian circles in which I moved to place a heavy emphasis on the individual words 'submission' and 'headship' and to ignore the setting in which these words are embedded, 'as to the Lord' and 'as Christ is the head of the church'. When this approach is adopted it is easy to deduce from Ephesians 5:22 ff. that the submissive wife is to remain in subjection to her husband, as subservient as the Jewish wife who actually called her husband 'master' and 'lord' (1 Pet. 3:6), and as servile as the women to whom Paul was writing. Implicit in much of the teaching I heard was the understanding that the wife was 'number two' and that 'her place was in the home'. I also gained the impression that a husband's headship gave him the right to make major family decisions and to bulldoze them through if necessary. After all, head meant 'ruler'. One mature Christian whom I respected told me that I 'belonged' to David in the sense that I was one of his possessions. But are wives chattels?

Like many women, when I was first married, I was shy and insecure. I felt inferior to my husband in every way. The acceptance of this so-called Christian teaching therefore presented few problems. On the contrary, I was relieved to assume a dependent rôle and I failed to see that dependency and submission are not one and the same; they contradict one another. As often happens in marriage, my husband's loving over the years has drawn out much of my latent ability, including the right use of my intellect; to think, to question, to challenge.

When Lee Ling questioned me about submission I had reached a state of personal confusion and turmoil. All I could do was indentify with her exasperated conclusion, 'I don't think I'll ever be a submissive wife.'

That conversation unsettled me. It pushed me into making a careful examination of the Bible's teaching on the subject. My personal findings are the fruit of years of groping towards a fuller and more accurate understanding of God's call to married couples. You must weigh them for yourselves as you decide what you are going to do with the question of submission, obedience, loving and headship in your own marriage.

Paul and his background
When Paul wrote his letter to the Ephesians, the incidence of

marital breakdown amongst Jews, Greeks and Romans had reached phenomenal proportions. Marriage exalted the husband to a lordly position and granted him extensive and tyrannical rights, while it depressed the wife's status to that of a slave. The husband's rights are reflected in Roman law. 'If you should take your wife in adultery, you may with impunity put her to death without a trial; but if you should commit adultery or indecency, she must not presume to lay a finger on you, nor does the law allow it.'[2] If a wife was discovered drinking wine she could be beaten to death by her husband.

Women in Greece were also held in bondage by the institution of marriage. A woman was never granted citizen status and enjoyed neither political nor legal rights. Marital rights for the Greek wife were few according to Demosthenes. He describes the wife whose responsibility was to provide her husband with an heir but who took no part in his social or domestic life. The Greek husband, meanwhile, centred his life either on the male world of the market place or on the sexual attractions of other women. 'Mistresses we keep for pleasure, concubines for daily attendance upon our person, wives to bear us legitimate children and to be our faithful house-keepers.'[3]

Jews also had a low view of women. In Jewish law a woman was not a person. She was a thing. Perhaps it is not surprising, therefore, that the Jews twisted the high view of marriage we read of in Deuteronomy 24:1, interpreting this verse in the broadest possible way. The more liberal rabbis claimed that this verse meant that a man might divorce his wife if she spoiled his dinner by putting too much salt in his food, if she walked in public with her head uncovered, if she talked with men in the streets, if she spoke disrespectfully to her husband's parents in her husband's hearing, if she was a brawling woman, if she was troublesome or quarrelsome. A certain Rabbi Akiba interpreted the phrase *if she find no favour in his sight* to mean that a husband might divorce his wife if he found a woman whom he considered more attractive.[4]

A Jewish wife, on the other hand, possessed few rights. She was permitted to sue for a divorce in three eventualities only.

First, if her husband became an apostate. Second, if he contracted leprosy. And third, if he engaged in a disgusting trade.

Paul's revolutionary teaching

When Paul wrote to the Ephesians and Colossians on the subject of marriage, he would have in mind women who may well have been disillusioned, uncomplaining and subservient. He was addressing men who expected to boss their wives around. He spoke about a relationship which had fallen into widespread disrepute. And with the directness and incisiveness of one who was inspired by the Lord he taught them a new basis for marriage. Marriage must no longer degenerate into a relationship which exploits inequality. On the contrary, Christian marriage must reflect to the watching world the love which exists between Christ, the heavenly bridegroom, and His bride, the church. The relationship Paul outlined for Christians was new. It would transform a decadent society. For converts to Christianity Paul's admonitions would have been mind-blowing. Somehow the wife who had become a Christian had to learn to emerge from the bondage in which society had imprisoned her. A new code of behaviour is placed before husbands. And Christian marriages gain a new master, the Lord Himself (Eph. 5:21).

In one sense Paul's teaching was not new. He was reiterating the teaching given to couples at Creation (Gn. 2:24); the same teaching in which Jesus emphasized God's original place for marriage (Mt. 19:5; Mk. 10:7–8).

This design seems to have involved the couple in partnership power over all living things. Socially, they seem to have been equal (Gn. 1:26–28). Couples were to enjoy sexual oneness (2:24), an egalitarian spiritual relationship in which both were blessed by God (1:26) and a procreative partnership (1:27). But Adam and Eve flaunted the divine intentions and through disobedience forfeited much of the marital enjoyment which God planned for them. But that which the first Adam destroyed, the second Adam, Christ, came to restore. Paul reminds the Christians in Galatia that 'there are no more distinctions between...male and female, but all of

43

you are one in Christ Jesus' (Gal. 3:28 JB).

The Bible's teaching to couples on equality and authority is anchored in paradox. On the one hand it underlines the sexual and spiritual equality of married people in acknowledging that they become 'one flesh' and that they are 'heirs together' of the Kingdom of God. On the other hand, it places before them the fact that the husband is the divinely appointed 'head' of the relationship (Eph. 5:23). Headship in a partnership of equality can only be understood when its nature has been examined. And Paul leaves Christians in no doubt concerning the style of headship which he is recommending. 'The husband is the head of the wife as Christ is the head of the church, his body, of which he is the Saviour' (5:23 NIV). Paul's emphasis here is not on the authority and power of Christ but on his self-giving: 'Husbands, love your wives, just at Christ loved the Church *and gave himself up for her*' (5:25 NIV). His own words to His disciples help us to understand His attitude: 'Whoever wants to become great among you must be your servant, and whoever wants to be first must be slave of all. For even the Son of Man did not come to be served, but to serve, and to give his life a ransom for many' (Mk. 10:43–45 NIV). The husband's headship, far from containing rights to be claimed, presents a superlative standard of self-sacrifice which leaves many Christian men asking, 'Who is equal to this task?'

The Bible makes a clear distinction between the contribution which husbands and wives are required to make to marriage. There is no hint of a unisex approach. The Christian husband is to love his wife in the same manner as Christ loved the church. The Christian wife, in addition to loving her husband (Tit. 2:4) is also required to submit to her husband (Eph. 5:22) and to obey him (1 Pet. 3:7). When the words 'love' and 'submit' are rightly understood, it becomes clear that *both* attitudes are a blow to human pride. The standard demanded of both partners is high. The outworkings of those standards will involve both partners in pain, self-renunciation and dedication. These are hard sayings. But Paul is not concerned here with comfortable feelings nor is he fighting the battle of the sexes. Rather he aims to pass on spiritual truths which are essential to the formation of healthy Christian marriages.

Paul's instructions to couples leave no scope for bargaining. So it is not permissible for the husband to promise to love his wife *if* she promises to submit. Similarly the wife is admonished to submit to her husband with no strings attached. Some women in the early church, like many wives today, found themselves 'unequally yoked' with a husband who was not a Christian. But it does not alter the divine order. The Christian wife is required to submit to her husband's leadership and to love him even if he does not love her with the high degree of loving which Paul prescribes.

Before you read on it is worth considering:

How do you feel about Paul's instructions?

Do you feel you or your partner has more to lose?

What will your marriage gain if you adhere to the standards before you?

Instructions to husbands

'Husbands, love your wives just as Christ loved the church and gave himself up for her' (Eph. 5:25 NIV).

When Paul instructs Christian husbands in the art of loving their wives, he makes it clear that the familiar picture of the tyrannical husband finds no place within a Christian framework. Harshness is forbidden (Col. 3:19). Paul's entire emphasis is on the duty a Christian husband has, because of his 'headship', to become his wife's self-forgetting companion. The husband's prototype is to be found in Jesus. The husband's main aim should be to emulate the love Christ demonstrates for His bride, the church. This kind of loving is not just an emotion; it is an orientation, a chain of choices, a series of actions which are planned to bring about the wife's well-being, happiness and ultimate wholeness.

The high cost of loving following the pattern Christ set includes an element of voluntary self-sacrifice (Eph. 5:25 JB). It hurts. But just as Jesus gave Himself up for His bride, 'He loved me and gave Himself up for me' (Gal. 2:20), just as His love stooped to wash His disciples' sweaty feet, so the Christian husband must be prepared to get his hands dirty by doing menial tasks and to feel the pain which is always interlocked with loving. John Powell outlines some of the implications of self-sacrificing love; 'Love implies that I am ready and willing to forego my own convenience, to invest my own time, and even to risk my own security to promote your satisfaction, security and development.'[5]

When a husband loves his wife in this way he draws out her full potential and Paul implies that this is another of the husband's duties (v. 26). Fulfilment of this duty is one of the greatest gifts a husband can give to his wife. It is liberating. It enables her to recognize her unique beauty and to acknowledge her own worth. A husband whose aim is to promote his wife will avoid 'putting her down', he will not try to 'score points' off her or make derisive comments about her. These are the antitheses of love. Rather he will find opportunities to affirm her and to sing her praise (Pr. 31:10).

Christ loves His bride not only when she is at her most lovely. 'God demonstrates his own love for us in this: While we were still sinners Christ died for us' (Rom. 5:8 NIV). Just as the bride of Christ is continuously on the receiving end of the undeserved goodness of the God who freely forgives her, so a Christian husband has to learn to forgive his wife, 'not seven times, but seventy times seven'. Forgiveness is the generosity which restores broken relationships. Forgiveness includes acceptance without acquiescence. It is the capacity to accept your wife as a person even when you cannot condone her actions. Forgiveness, as Neville Ward puts it, is the ability a person has to bear 'injury without retaliation and without his love becoming even just a little frightened and therefore more cautious and reserved, so that there is now simply a richer love where that evil has been done.'[6]

Christ's love is an unbreakable love. John Powell describes unbreakable love in this way: 'I will always be there for you. Effective love is not like the retractable point on a ballpoint pen. If I say I am your man, I will always be your man.'[7] God says the same thing in another way when He reminds Israel, 'I have loved you with an everlasting love' (Je. 31:3), and Jesus repeats the message of unending love, 'As the Father has loved me, so have I loved you' (Jn. 15:9).

46

Christ's love is not a weak, spineless thing. He refuses to dilute what He knows to be the Father's will. His relationship with His bride includes tender, incisive, accurate, powerful, God-given commands. 'Follow me' (Mt. 4:19), 'Ask...seek ...knock' (Mt. 7:7), 'Go' (Mt. 8:13). The reason why Jesus was free to demonstrate such fearless authority was three-fold. First, He Himself was a person content to be under submission to His Father (Jn. 14:31). Second, He learned to bring His own will into complete alignment with His Father's (Lk. 22:42). And third, He did not issue self-centred commands or even utter His own words. All His plans originated in His Father (Jn. 14:10). When Christian men today similarly use their God-given authority with sensitivity, they earn the respect which is their due (Eph. 5:33). In the climate in which we live, maybe the responsibility to give a Christ-like lead is the most difficult duty which Christian husbands have to learn to fulfil. But I speak as a woman!

Which of these duties do you feel it will be hardest for you *to carry out?*

Instructions to wives
'Wives submit to your husbands as to the Lord' (Eph. 5:22).

I have spent hours studying this passage in Ephesians. I placed it in context, approached each verse with objectivity and thought that, at last, I understood what was required of a submissive wife. But when I copied out v.22 just now, I became aware of a wriggling and a squirming and a struggling inside me. Clearly, my emotions and my intellect are not entirely disentangled. And this entanglement is one of the chief obstacles many women meet as they approach this subject. Many have spoken to me of the negative emotions which are stirred up in them by the mere mention of the words 'submit' and 'obey'. Christian men may plead, 'Really to lose the self for another is probably harder for the male who is brought up to be self-sufficient', but the concept of self-renunciation is as uncomfortable for most women as it is for men. For this reason some Christian women today are refusing to include the promise 'to obey' in the wedding service.

The uncomfortable feelings must be listened to because they reveal a great deal about ourselves. But life consists of more than feelings. The Christian life is about facts as well as feelings, about obedience as well as need.

Some women fear that if they agree to submit, they will become doormats, 'yes' women. But the husband's headship does not grant him the right to keep his wife under his thumb. On the contrary, Christian marriage liberates women.

Women who feel insulted by the mention of the word 'submission' often misunderstand its true meaning. So their pride is injured. Others react defensively because they feel that submission will limit their preoccupation with self, self-interest, self-fulfilment, self-indulgence. But pride and selfishness are sins to be confessed. They are not weapons with which Christians fight for so-called rights.

The submission question sometimes presses on the doubts we women nurse about our own worth. We are afraid of being labelled 'inferior' because we fear that the label might be accurate. We go to great lengths therefore, to mask those fears, to camouflage them with a pseudo-identity which is dependent on what we *do* rather than who we are. But the Christian woman is assured that her value is secured in Christ and His love for her. The Christian gospel makes it clear that woman is not inferior to man. Men and women are both God's masterpieces (Gn. 1:31).

Women today who do recognize their worth may reject the injunction to submit for a different reason. Their rejection is a reaction against those Christian women who become insipid non-persons out of false humility. They know that Christianity does not seek to keep women in subjection. On the contrary, it was Christ who raised the status of women from the level of chattels to the position of persons. It was Jesus who invited women to accompany Him (Lk. 8:1–3) and to minister to Him (Jn. 12:1–7). He healed women (Lk. 13:10–13), imparted spiritual truths to them (Jn. 11:25) and used them and their work to illustrate the nature of His kingdom (Lk. 13:20–21). Jesus' revolutionary attitude towards women should allay some of the fears we women harbour. His up-grading of the status of women leads to a more accurate

This submissive wife did not restrict her activities to her home and family. Her abilities spilled over into the circles in which she moved. This fulfilled, creative, strong woman whose talents were channelled to promote her husband, her children and the needy made a significant contribution to the society in which she lived. In submitting, she received much praise.

This attractive picture of submission need not be fantasy. We have proved the value of attempting to interact in this way in our own marriage. When I resist the temptation to go my own selfish way, and volutarily donate my insights, my personal strengths and my talents to David, our complementarity produces a strong team. I now know that David wants me alongside him, not to boss me around, but because he respects me and is asking for the contributions which he knows I can make. This is not degrading. It is rewarding. The thrilling thing is that after twenty years of being on the receiving end of his loving, I have so much more to yield to him now than when we were first married.

Mutual self-offering

And so we return to the mystery of two equal persons intertwined with one another as partners while acknowledging that the husband is the chief among equals. C. S. Lewis points out the importance of establishing this order of headship and obedience in marriage:

> As long as the husband and wife are agreed, no question of a head need arise; and we may hope that this will be the normal state of affairs in a Christian marriage. But when there is real disagreement what is to happen? Talk it over, of course: but I am assuming they have done that and still failed to reach agreement. What do they do next?…in a council of two there can be no majority. Surely only one or other of two things can happen: either they must separate and go their own ways or else one or other of them must have a casting vote. If marriage is permanent, one or other party must, in the last resort, have the power of deciding the family policy. You cannot have a permanent association without a constitution.[9]

I think that is what Peter meant
obey their husbands (1 Pet. 3:1–
the wife permission to leave all
husband. That is servility. The
of the Christian wife involves her
feels, believes and thinks. The lo
Christian husband requires tha
wife, weighs what she has said,
concerned for her well-being. If h
then she must trust him and st
appears to have made the wrong

I am not suggesting that obedi
But the fact that something is diffi
Most of us have to learn the art of
encouragement from the reminde
to obey through suffering' (Heb.

There is a danger of giving the i
question represents a serious prob
I reflect on our own relationship,
because our moments of stalema
we did reach serious deadlock. D
Rector of St Nicholas' Church
went to see the church, we were
had divided the congregation. V
rectory which stands on the city's
warned that tramps could be a
were particularly troublesome
shuddered at the thought of liv
noisy house with two small chil
hand, began to grow excited b
which existed in that place. We
and our conclusions did not c
decision to the Lord and I like to t
me to say my 'yes'. Indeed, I
necessary grace to bring my will i
even if He hadn't, in the light of
submission in marriage, I believ
'yes' as my response to David's l
all, my happiness and well-being

God
relation
No mar
loves th
whole s
strength
optimis
that 'wi

It is
women
submit
the rew
grasped
self-offe
and wh

Notes

1. Jack
2. Quot
   (Font
3. Ibid.,
4. Infor
   (St A
5. John
6. Nevi
7. John
8. Isaac
9. C. S.

What are your feelings about having children?

Preparing for parenthood

Since starting a family precipitates so many changes, a couple is wise to be aware of the careful preparations which they can make. The physical changes in the mother might leave her feeling robust, healthy, with more vitality than usual; on the other hand she might feel tired, lethargic and sick. As the wife learns to adjust to the physical, emotional and hormonal changes taking place within herself, the husband also has to settle for a wife who may become hypersensitive, less interested in sexual activity and more reflective in personality. At times of acute change in life most people need a great deal of support, and the mysterious months when a foetus is growing as a result of your love is a time when your marriage undergoes a remoulding. It is a time therefore for extra tenderness, increased cherishing and especial care.

You also need to be prepared spiritually. The Psalmist was conscious that he was formed in the womb by God (see Ps. 139). As you pray for your unborn child God acts on behalf of him/her and He also does a transforming work within both of you. He prepares you for the miracle of giving birth and the hard work of bringing up that child for Him.

The practical preparations, buying nappies, choosing a pram, decorating a nursery, are great fun but there are financial challenges to be met. If you have both been working, the future of the wife's career or profession must be faced. Some couples, while feeling that they both want children, find it equally hard to imagine the wife abandoning her career. The women's liberation movement claims that it is unfair to the woman to expect her to abdicate her profession, to deprive society of the capabilities of educated women. They demand that every opportunity should be granted to women to facilitate an early return to work after childbirth.

As a professional woman with a strong career bias, I would want to argue the case for women recognizing that motherhood is a calling which requires sacrifice, and that babies are born with a need for love which a mother-substitute cannot adequately supply. I have seen the strain on our family when

67

interpretation of the injunction which we cannot erase: 'Wives submit to your husbands as to the Lord.'

'As to the Lord.' That phrase contains the key to an accurate understanding of what Paul is asking of Christian wives. The women who accompanied Jesus were devoted to Him. Some of them expressed their devotion by lingering at the cross. Some of them came early to the tomb on Easter Day. They brought expensive spices to embalm His body. These women loved the Lord so much that they sacrificed time, energy, emotion, money, sleep and reputation for the sake of His well-being. And that is what submission is. Submission is not being held in subjection from terror. It is a positive, deliberate, voluntary donation of all you have and are for the well-being of another. Submission is the inward compulsion of love in response to love. Paul expressed it well when he declared, out of love for Christ, 'Whatever was to my profit I now consider loss for the sake of Christ. What is more, I consider everything a loss compared to the surpassing greatness of knowing Christ Jesus my Lord, for whose sake I have lost all things. I consider them rubbish, that I may gain Christ and be found in him...' (Phil. 3:7–9 NIV). A hymn-writer sums it all up in two lines:

Love so amazing, so divine
Demands my soul, my life, my all.[8]

Submission, then, is a privilege and can be enjoyable!

The book of Proverbs presents us with a picture of a gifted married woman who seems to have enjoyed submitting herself to her husband. This 'perfect wife' (Pr. 31:10 ff.) certainly did not pretend that she had no strengths. She appears to have been, among other things, an accomplished needle-woman, a shrewd administrator and a successful business woman. She seems to have possessed boundless energy, a compassionate nature and a discerning mind. The narrative implies that she voluntarily invested all of these strengths in her husband's welfare. She did not lose her personal identity or become overwhelmed by him. They interacted as two autonomous people. She provided him with mental stimulus, and clearly he admired and respected her.

This submissive wife did not restrict her activities to her home and family. Her abilities spilled over into the circles in which she moved. This fulfilled, creative, strong woman whose talents were channelled to promote her husband, her children and the needy made a significant contribution to the society in which she lived. In submitting, she received much praise.

This attractive picture of submission need not be fantasy. We have proved the value of attempting to interact in this way in our own marriage. When I resist the temptation to go my own selfish way, and voluntarily donate my insights, my personal strengths and my talents to David, our complementarity produces a strong team. I now know that David wants me alongside him, not to boss me around, but because he respects me and is asking for the contributions which he knows I can make. This is not degrading. It is rewarding. The thrilling thing is that after twenty years of being on the receiving end of his loving, I have so much more to yield to him now than when we were first married.

Mutual self-offering

And so we return to the mystery of two equal persons intertwined with one another as partners while acknowledging that the husband is the chief among equals. C. S. Lewis points out the importance of establishing this order of headship and obedience in marriage:

> As long as the husband and wife are agreed, no question of a head need arise; and we may hope that this will be the normal state of affairs in a Christian marriage. But when there is real disagreement what is to happen? Talk it over, of course: but I am assuming they have done that and still failed to reach agreement. What do they do next?...in a council of two there can be no majority. Surely only one or other of two things can happen: either they must separate and go their own ways or else one or other of them must have a casting vote. If marriage is permanent, one or other party must, in the last resort, have the power of deciding the family policy. You cannot have a permanent association without a constitution.[9]

I think that is what Peter meant when he challenged wives to obey their husbands (1 Pet. 3:1–6). Obedience does not give the wife permission to leave all the decision-making to her husband. That is servility. The obedience which is required of the Christian wife involves her in stating clearly what she feels, believes and thinks. The loving which is demanded of a Christian husband requires that he listens carefully to his wife, weighs what she has said, listens to the Lord and is concerned for her well-being. If he and his wife cannot agree, then she must trust him and stand by him even when he appears to have made the wrong decision!

I am not suggesting that obedience is easy for most women. But the fact that something is difficult does not make it wrong. Most of us have to learn the art of obedience and we may find encouragement from the reminder that even our Lord 'learnt to obey through suffering' (Heb. 5:8 JB).

There is a danger of giving the impression that the obedience question represents a serious problem for most couples. When I reflect on our own relationship, it scarcely even troubles us because our moments of stalemate are rare. Eight years ago we did reach serious deadlock. David was invited to become Rector of St Nicholas' Church in Nottingham. When we went to see the church, we were told of the problems which had divided the congregation. We were shown the isolated rectory which stands on the city's inner by-pass and we were warned that tramps could be a problem and drunken men were particularly troublesome on Saturday evenings. I shuddered at the thought of living in that isolated, dirty, noisy house with two small children. David, on the other hand, began to grow excited by the potential for growth which existed in that place. We both expressed our feelings and our conclusions did not coincide. We submitted the decision to the Lord and I like to think it was He who enabled me to say my 'yes'. Indeed, I believe He did grant the necessary grace to bring my will into alignment with His. But even if He hadn't, in the light of my study on authority and submission in marriage, I believe I should have had to say 'yes' as my response to David's leadership under God. After all, my happiness and well-being is their affair and not mine.

God granted the necessary grace. Marriage is a demanding relationship. The standards set in this chapter are impossible. No man can hope to love his wife in the same way as Christ loves the church. And no woman can hope to donate her whole self to her husband. Both must receive from God the strength which they each need. In this strength lies our optimism for we who know Christ also have the assurance that 'with God all things are possible' (Mt. 19:26).

It is therefore to be regretted that few contemporary women in the west today marry with the notion of obeying or submitting to their husbands. They deny themselves many of the rewards which self-giving affords. It is sad that equality is grasped when it is something to be received; a basis of the self-offering which husbands and wives make to one another and which enriches both.

Notes for chapter six

1. Jack Dominian, *Authority* (Darton, Longman and Todd, 1976), p.69.
2. Quoted by Julia O'Faolain and Lauro Martines (eds.), *Not in God's Image* (Fontana, 1974), p.27.
3. *Ibid.*, p.55.
4. Information from William Barclay, *The Letter to the Galatians and Ephesians* (St Andrew Press, 1966), p.200.
5. John Powell, *The Secret of Staying in Love* (Argus, 1974), p.53.
6. Neville Ward, *Friday Afternoon* (Epworth, no date), p.19.
7. John Powell, *The Secret of Staying in Love* (Argus, 1974), p.44.
8. Isaac Watts, 'When I survey the wondrous cross'.
9. C. S. Lewis, *Mere Christianity* (Geoffrey Bles, 1969), p.88.

7 Partners in Prayer

The story is told of an old man who lived in France whose life was disciplined and predictable. Each morning saw him walking to the small chapel in the village where he lived and there he would sit for an hour or more, silent, unaware that he was being watched by the priest. One morning the Curé d'Ars determined to ask the old man why he came to the chapel and what he did as he sat motionless in the pew. The saintly peasant simply replied, 'I look at Him and He looks at me, and we tell each other that we love each other.' Over the years, this man had discovered that prayer is to life what the roots are to a tree. Prayer brings stability and transmits nourishment to a person throughout the changes of life. He therefore made prayer a top priority each day.

Most Christians pay lip-service to the desirability, even the necessity of spending time alone each day with God, but, as Stephen Doyle observes, 'If people were asked, "Do you have a relationship with Jesus?" most Christians would answer "yes". If they were asked, "When did you last talk with Him?" most would have difficulty in answering.'[1] If this is true of individuals, it is even more true of married couples. I recently asked a dozen couples, 'How important is prayer to your marriage?' They replied, 'It's very important.' But when I asked, 'How often do you pray together?' with the exception of one couple, they all replied, 'Hardly ever'. This inconsistency between our belief and our way of life leads to impoverishment. Prayer enriches relationships.

Alice Gavoty, the wife of a French diplomat, records in her diary how shared prayer with her husband Joseph enhanced their joy in one another and in God. 'From the start we used to say our prayers together…We found the Lord more and more in each other and we regarded this as the blessing on our union which He had willed. Near Joseph, I almost always had an actual sense of God's presence.'[2] A young couple who wrote to me soon after their wedding were finding something similar: 'We are already excited by what we are learning about praying together.' As I reflect on our own marriage I recall that the most harmonious patches are those where we pray together with regularity, method and perseverance. It is as the nineteenth century Bishop Theophan says, 'Prayer is the test of everything. If prayer is right, everything is right.'

'When we are married, should we pray together or alone?' The questioners were an engaged couple who wanted to become partners in prayer without losing the personal encounter with God which was important to each of them. There is no answer to that question because just as each person's relationship with God is unique, so each partnership will approach prayer in a unique way. The Bible clearly states that there is a place for both kinds of prayer within marriage. In 1 Samuel we read how Hannah approached God alone and made the blunt request for a son. But after Samuel's birth, it is Hannah and Elkanah together who come to God to offer worship and thanksgiving. Similarly, Mary and Joseph during their betrothal period, were met by God separately, but after the birth of Jesus, they attended the temple together. Togetherness in prayer is important. And shared prayer is fed by the *individual's* encounter with God.

Both kinds of prayer are fed by a study of the Bible. In fact, Christian prayer is rooted in the Word of God. How can we hope to listen to God unless we know who He is and what He said?

Turning Godwards together

Bible reading and prayer are sometimes placed before us as duties to perform. But they are not merely duties. They are an adventure. As Archbishop Anthony Bloom expresses it, prayer is 'that moment when you turn Godwards', it is that moment when you recognize the truth of James. 4:8, that as you draw near to God, taking but one faltering step towards Him, He is already drawing near to you. This is true of individuals, and of partners in prayer. The couple who walked disconsolately along the road to Emmaus on the first Easter Sunday (Lk. 24:13–32) discovered this vital truth. Heavy-hearted, disillusioned, confused, they poured out their grief to their unknown companion. Little by little He unfolded the truth to them and then, in a flash of inspiration, reality dawned. This happens in prayer too. Sharing our problems together and with Him we meet the Lord, and our confusion is melted in knowing Him.

Prayer is exciting, too, because when Christians pray together miracles happen. Behind Peter's release from prison (Acts 12:1–17) was a group of Christians in prayer. Shared prayer preceded Pentecost. The Welsh revival of 1905 was anticipated by Christians praying together. Couples praying in partnership have unwittingly influenced the world. André Louf, for example, dedicates his book *Teach us to Pray*, 'For mother and father whom I frequently saw at prayer and from whom I learned to pray.' As Ralph Martin expresses it, 'prayer is not a pious addition to things…it is a force allowing things to happen which could not have occurred without it.'

Prayer is an adventure because prayer is the work of God's Spirit within us (Rom. 8) and as Peter Hocken puts it, 'The Spirit makes fresh what has become stale, puts new flesh on old bones, and causes new life to pulse through the old body.'[3]

Couples who pray together reap a personal advantage. They keep short accounts with one another and with God. It is impossible to pray with someone whom you refuse to forgive. Prayer, therefore, is a great leveller. In prayer both partners stand before one another and God, 'sinful, spiritually handicapped and disabled in many ways, chronic patients. And we accept these handicaps and disabilities because He accepts us as we are, and because He loves us as we are.'[4]

We are accepted by God, not because it's good for us to be as we are but because Jesus died to secure our forgiveness and reconciliation. If 'while we were yet sinners, Christ died for us' (Rom. 6:8) surely we must accept each other. A person who accepts himself as he is and his partner as she is because God

55

accepts them both is on the pathway to wholeness.

As we learn to expose the hurt we all suffer to one another and to God, we are not the only ones to benefit. Through prayer, God enables us to become instruments of peace to others and vehicles of healing to one another.

As St Francis of Assisi puts it:

Lord,
Make me an instrument of your peace.
Where there is hatred, let me show love;
Where there is injury, pardon;
Where there is doubt, faith;
Where there is despair, hope;
Where there is darkness, light;
And where there is sadness, joy.

Problems in prayer

Couples who pray together embark on a fulfilling spiritual life. I have to confess, however, that prayer together poses problems in our marriage. Praying together is often a struggle. We frequently neglect it and there have been many occasions when God has seemed more absent than present in our relationship simply because we have not bothered to seek Him. Others, too, have spoken to me of the problems they face when they attempt to pray together.

There is the problem of considering prayer merely as a duty: 'We feel we ought to pray together and feel terribly guilty because we don't. It even takes a lot of courage to admit in Christian circles that we don't find it helpful to pray together.'

There is the problem of familiarity: 'It all becomes so ludicrous so what *is* the point?'

There is the problem of intolerance: 'I can't bear Ron's intensity and the way he uses jargon which he wouldn't use in normal conversation, so I'd much rather pray on my own, thank you very much.'

There is the problem of inadequacy when one partner or both prefer to avoid praying together in order to cover up feelings of insecurity. Take George for example. As a young Christian he felt angry because his wife refused to take a strong spiritual lead: 'She's a more mature Christian than I

56

am and I feel terribly let down because she doesn't take the initiative and suggest we pray together.' Ironically, his wife told me of her longing that they should pray together. She hesitated to suggest it because she didn't know how they would go about it.

There are also problems of laziness, indiscipline, apathy.

The paradox about prayer is that it is both a gift from God through the Holy Spirit (Rom. 8:26) and at the same time it is an art to be learned. As a gift, it must be received. Couples also need to experiment with prayer. There is no need for anxiety. When we become over-anxious about technique in prayer we become like the centipede:

> A centipede was happy quite
> Until a frog in fun
> Said, "Pray, which leg comes after which?"
> This raised her mind to such a pitch,
> She lay distracted in a ditch,
> Considering how to run.[5]

Prayer is not a technique. It is a progression, 'from depth to depth, from height to height...at every step we already possess something which is rich, which is deep, and yet always go on longing for and moving towards something richer and deeper; it is why prayer is an insatiable hunger so that we must learn that there is always more.'[6]

Some methods of praying together

Partnership in prayer involves a three-fold activity, the partnership of praying *with* another person, of praying *for* that person and the partnership of 'just being' in the presence of God together. Praying with another person requires the discipline of an agreement, a time and a place. Praying for that person involves intercession, while 'just being' introduces an altogether different dimension of prayer into the relationship.

If you are serious about your desire to work at praying together, it will involve careful planning of time, for, as Ralph Martin reminds us, 'the demands of modern living are such that if we don't have a schedule for prayer, we probably won't pray.' Some couples like to begin each day with a few minutes of prayer together. Some commit five minutes each day to God and if they pray for longer, that is a love-offering over and above the covenant they have made. Others find that last thing at night is a better time for them, while some prefer to set aside an hour a week for more concentrated, leisurely prayer and Bible study.

Which is the best time for you to pray together?

Is it better for you to pray for a few minutes each day or for a longer period each week?

Where will you pray together? A place where you both feel relaxed and which is remote from the telephone is a valuable aid to concentration in prayer. In addition to an agreement, a time and a place you will need courage, perseverance and flexibility. 'To abandon prayer is equivalent to suicide in the physical life; to regard prayer as unchanging and without need of development is equivalent to being a fixed adolescent.'[7]

Our instructor in the art of praying is Jesus. Clearly there were times when prayer, for Him, was a spontaneous over-flow of the feelings which welled up inside Him. At the grave of Lazarus He uttered a prayer of trust: 'Father, I thank you that you have heard me' (Jn. 11:41 NIV). In Gethsemane He anguished in prayer: 'Father, if you are willing, remove this cup from me' (Lk. 22:42 NIV). There are occasions in our prayer life together when spontaneous prayer, called out of us by an awareness of God, will be appropriate.

Jesus also used 'ready-made prayers'. On the cross He prayed, 'My God, my God why have you forsaken me?' This is a prayer from Psalm 22:1. There will be occasions in our prayer partnership when one or both partners will prefer to use prayers written by other people. We, too, might pray the words of a Psalm; we might use the prayer of St Francis quoted earlier in this chapter, or one of the prayers reflecting modern pressures written by Michel Quoist in his book, *Prayers of life*. To pray in this way is not second best, or our Lord would not have resorted to the method. It is as Anthony Bloom says, 'If we imagine we can sustain spontaneous prayer throughout our life, we are in a childish delusion. Spontaneous prayer must gush out of our souls, we cannot simply turn on a tap and get it out...It comes from the depths of our soul, from either wonder or distress, but it does not come from the middle situation in which we are neither overwhelmed by the divine presence nor overwhelmed by a sense of who we are or the position in which we are...But when you cannot pray with spontaneity, you can still pray with conviction.'[8]

This conviction includes intercessory prayer. Sometimes, when interceding, it is sufficient to recognize the attentive presence of Christ and silently to hold into that presence those people or circumstances for which you are burdened. If we assume that an all-knowing God has no need for our advice or guidance but does somehow require our persistent prayer, we can dispense with vain repetition, abandon words and, like the friends of the paralytic (Lk. 5:17–26), who simply laid their friend before the Lord, we may do likewise. When together you 'hold' relatives, friends or circumstances in the presence of God, you hold them in the presence of love, for God is love; of power, for He is omnipotent, and of forgiveness, for unending forgiveness is what God is.

When you learn to pray in this way, your prayer overflows and penetrates your life together. Some couples I know listen to the news together and as they do so, silently, almost automatically, hold each crisis situation to God in prayer. There is no break in the daily routine but there is that united sense that God is there and in control. Others find it helpful to pray together as they work. One couple, for example, work in the garden alongside each other and as they do so, pray silently for an agreed person or situation. They then discover that prayer is an energy which binds couples together in a love-work partnership. They discover the truth of Carlo Carretto's words: 'There is something much greater than human action; prayer – and that it has a power much stronger than the words of men: love.'[9]

When the disciples observed Jesus at prayer, they said, 'Lord, teach us to pray.' As married people, we cannot repeat that prayer too often. As you make that request at the beginning of your marriage you might find it helpful to discuss:

Which method of prayer do I find most helpful: spontaneous prayer, extempore prayer, ready-made prayers or silent prayer?

How can we make prayer the axis of our marriage?

59

What action are we going to take now?

Notes for chapter seven

1. Quoted by Mark Link, *You* (Argus, 1976), p.94.
2. Quoted by Carlo Carretto, *Made in Heaven* (Darton, Longman and Todd, 1978), p.57.
3. Peter Hocken, *You He Made Alive* (Darton, Longman and Todd, 1974), p.7.
4. James Borst, *A Method of Contemplative Prayer* (Aslan Trading Corporation, 1973), p.14.
5. Anon, 'To a centipede and his hundred legs', *Arrow Book of Funny Poems* (Arrow, 1975), p.28.
6. Anthony Bloom, *School for Prayer* (Libra, 1974), p.13.
7. M. Mary Clare, *Encountering the Depths* (S.L.G., 1974), p.7.
8. Anthony Bloom, *op.cit.*, p.27.
9. Quoted by M. Mary Clare, *op.cit.*, p.15.

8 Marriage Is for Fruitfulness

I wonder what it will be,
What will come forth of us.
What flower, my love?
No matter, I am so happy,
I feel like a firm, rich, healthy root,
Rejoicing in what is to come...
There will something come forth from us.
Children, acts, utterance,
Perhaps only happiness.
Perhaps only happiness will come forth from us.
Old sorrow, and new happiness...[1]

In this poem, the author, though not writing from a Christian perspective, captures something of the wonder of fruitfulness in marriage. He shows that new life together must give birth to someone or something, and he highlights the joy couples can experience in investing themselves in children, caring and cherishing.

The teaching of the Bible and the discoveries of marriage counsellors coincide in emphasizing that wholesome closeness between couples is directly related to the concerns and relationships which exist *beyond* their partnership.

Some newly-weds, inebriated with marital love, are in danger of marital idolatry. Their homes and their relationship become the thing they 'worship'. In the early days of marriage bliss this is understandable but it is not Christian. It is the message of the world that we live for self-fulfilment, the gospel of the twentieth century that marriage fulfilment is the top priority. It is the selfishness and the magnetism of a gadget-oriented society which persuade us to over-indulge in our home-making.

Pleasing Him

Christian men and women have a bigger, more exciting goal than self-fulfilment, marriage fulfilment, even home-making. To use Paul's words, the mission for Christian couples, as for individuals, is to please Him who called us with a unique (holy) calling (2 Tim. 1:9). It is to minister for Him so that through your marriage God might be glorified. The top priority for Christians is to seek first the Kingdom of God, allowing Him to add the other things to us in His way and His time (Mt. 6:25–34). I am not saying that home-making is unimportant but I am saying that Jesus teaches that it is those who would cling to their lives who end up losing them, while it is those who are prepared to sacrifice who are enriched.

The highest pattern of love placed before us is that between Jesus and His heavenly Father. The divine partnership extends to embrace the whole of mankind (see Jn.17). Paul's partnership with God so changed his life that he too became one who could offer to others the same kind of consolation which he had received (2 Cor. 1). And so it is in healthy marriages, for 'creative intimacy in the home is the launching pad and propellant which allows one to orbit effectively outside the home.'[2]

Married couples in the Bible demonstrate this. The couple described in Proverbs 31:10–31, for example, involved themselves outside the family by exercising a caring ministry. In every city, in the suburbs and in many villages today, there are transplanted people who are rootless, restless, searching for a place to belong. The hospitality of a home, however simple, with its warmth and welcome, sometimes determines whether the uprooted grow stronger or suffer an inner, emotional death.

Are there young professionals, students or newcomers in your church or neighbourhood?

What might you as a couple do to provide them with the kind of relationship which satisfies their need?

How might you exercise a caring ministry?

Aquila and Priscilla were a couple who cared for others. It was they who gave shelter and encouragement to Paul. They also taught the famous Apollos who influenced countless people for Christ. And it was their home which became headquarters for an embryonic church in Ephesus. Your home too might become the centre for a small group meeting where other Christians come to share personal needs, to study the Bible or to pray. People often learn to pray and draw closer to others in the informality of a small meeting in a home rather than in a vast church building.

How are you planning to use your home? What are your feelings about opening its doors to others?

Reaching out

One purpose of marriage is to reach out to others. This reaching out is always costly.

When the divine love embraced the world, it cost the Father His only Son and it cost the Son His life. Effective Christian ministry is costly in terms of time, energy and emotion. A wise couple counts the cost and ensures that the balance between nurturing the marriage and output from the marriage is satisfactory for both partners. They recognize that God is no man's debtor, that when we give anything to Him, He reimburses us from the wealth of His own resources.

I think of one young couple who opened their home every Sunday to students and 'homeless' single people. They would always cook for more than their family in case a newcomer attended church. There would always be a house full of people on a Sunday afternoon. As their family grew and the fifth child was born they could ill afford the money, the inroads on their privacy or the battering to their furniture which such demanding hospitality involved but they viewed these as love-offerings for Christ. I remember the wife speaking to me of the joy they experienced as they watched lonely people gradually find their feet in a strange town. She spoke of the thrill of seeing young people searching for Christ and finding Him in their home. Many of 'the regulars' adopted her family as their own, loved them, prayed for them and supported them.

Thus, a cycle of loving was formed which seemed to have no beginning and no ending. The couple poured out love at great cost, but God replenished their resources with His own blessing. And, of course, they were never short of baby-sitters. Their children were enriched by a variety of 'uncles and aunties'. The home was a place of laughter and joy.

Not all couples possess this kind of resilience. But there is a quieter contribution they can make. It is unseen by the world, but not unknown to God. One couple, for example, write regularly to one of our missionaries, send her anonymous food parcels and pray for her through many crises.

Are you willing to be used by God? If so, you might find the following questions helpful:

Which pressing needs in the church or our neighbourhood arouse our interest? What is required to alleviate that need?

What are our combined resources? Where might we have maximum opportunity to use those gifts to good effect?

Is there someone living locally who might appreciate the hospitality of our home? If we become involved in this way, what will the cost be to our marrriage?

Do we both believe that if we seek first the Kingdom of God through our marriage, He will add to us all that is necessary? If so, are we prepared to act?

Be fruitful and multiply

I like going abroad. I find it fascinating to discover familiar foods labelled with 'foreign' names and thrilling to adjust to a different way of life. When you are abroad you are the same, yet different. Similarly, when a baby arrives, a couple remains the same yet they find that life has an added dimension. Marriage does not necessarily need the addition of children and yet the Bible, the marriage service and human instinct anticipate children. At creation, God commanded Adam and Eve to have children. In Old Testament times childless couples were despised, and many Bible references indicate that children are to be considered a blessing, a joy, even a reward from God (*e.g.* Ps. 127:3–5).

If you marry in an Anglican church, there will be a prayer asking God to grant you the gift of children. It is assumed

64

that when your love has ripened and deepened that you will both want children. The presupposition is that marriage is for procreation and that most couples will find their ultimate satisfaction in the fruitfulness of child-bearing.

But many couples have spoken to me of the fears which overshadow them as they contemplate parenthood. There is the fear of taking the plunge, the problem of deciding when to start a family or indeed, whether they ought to bring children into a decaying world at all.

Then what about those who *cannot* have children? Couples who are entrusted with childlessness need not be denied the privilege and responsibility of creating new persons. The fruitfulness of childless marriages might still revolve around the little people who will be adopted or fostered. But fruitfulness may involve not creating new lives so much as re-creating damaged ones. The uprooted people I mentioned earlier, together with broken and troubled persons, search for a sensitive touch in the brash, fast-moving world in which we live. Couples who have worked through the disappointment of childlessness with Christ, and who have allowed Him to touch this particular wound, often find themselves equipped to bind up the sores of others who also encounter deprivation and loss. The enhanced sensitivity gained itself becomes a source of fruitfulness.

On the other hand, with reliable contraception freely available, some couples who *can* have children are in danger of devaluing the addition of a child. Is a baby a *thing* which a man and woman create? Or is a baby a gift from God? Babies are persons. Parenthood is about person-making. Child-rearing is a demanding vocation, but God gives couples who ask Him the ability to love, to train and to discipline children. It is one of the most thrilling, challenging and exacting 'projects' of marriage, but the ability to become good parents does not come naturally. It does come as a step-by-step growth into a vocation which demands the combined resources of both partners.

Some couples are more careless about creating new lives than chefs are about creating special dishes. Yet when you decide to cook a special meal, you carefully select the necessary

65

ingredients. Good parenting also needs certain ingredients. The presence of felt love between the parents is required. There should also be the ability to respond to physical, spiritual and practical changes within the relationship. A growing child not only needs to be loved by both father and mother, he/she also needs to perceive the love the parents have for one another. When parents demonstrate their love for one another as well as for their offspring, childhood is like walking underneath an avenue of beech trees in summer; it is a sheltered place, a place of beauty, and in its protection there is freedom. When parents fail to merge, perhaps un-noticed, over the lives of their young, or worse, when they openly quarrel, their children frequently show lasting signs of insecurity and fear. They begin to doubt their own self-worth.

When is the best time to have a baby? The strong bias towards selfishness which characterizes most of us requires careful and patient unlearning and most couples find that, during the first two years of marriage, considerable adjust-ments need to be made. During these months, you discover the frightening truth that you have married someone as sinful, inconsiderate and self-centred as yourself. It follows, therefore, that if you are to offer your first child a well-adjusted, mature love, it is wise to wait for a year, or maybe two, before giving birth to your first baby.

Some counsellors feel that an older woman makes a better mother than a young wife. This may well be true but do not wait too long. There are risks in postponing your first child beyond the wife's thirtieth birthday. Moreover, many couples would find it frustrating to wait that long. The financial pull, that strong deterrent to starting a family when you grow accustomed to living on two salaries, is another factor. It could dissuade you from receiving God's gift of a child even though you are ready. There is no right or wrong time for a couple to start a family. It is not a disaster if you conceive within the first year of marriage, neither is it a catastrophe if you wait, though for some couples 'when we are really ready' may mean never!

How do you feel about the timing in your particular circumstances? Lay your hopes and fears before the Lord for His overruling

Preparing for parenthood

Since starting a family precipitates so many changes, a couple is wise to be aware of the careful preparations which they can make. The physical changes in the mother might leave her feeling robust, healthy, with more vitality than usual; on the other hand she might feel tired, lethargic and sick. As the wife learns to adjust to the physical, emotional and hormonal changes taking place within herself, the husband also has to settle for a wife who may become hypersensitive, less interested in sexual activity and more reflective in personality. At times of acute change in life most people need a great deal of support, and the mysterious months when a foetus is growing as a result of your love is a time when your marriage undergoes a remoulding. It is a time therefore for extra tenderness, increased cherishing and especial care.

You also need to be prepared spiritually. The Psalmist was conscious that he was formed in the womb by God (see Ps. 139). As you pray for your unborn child God acts on behalf of him/her and He also does a transforming work within both of you. He prepares you for the miracle of giving birth and the hard work of bringing up that child for Him.

The practical preparations, buying nappies, choosing a pram, decorating a nursery, are great fun but there are financial challenges to be met. If you have both been working, the future of the wife's career or profession must be faced. Some couples, while feeling that they both want children, find it equally hard to imagine the wife abandoning her career. The women's liberation movement claims that it is unfair to the woman to expect her to abdicate her profession, to deprive society of the capabilities of educated women. They demand that every opportunity should be granted to women to facilitate an early return to work after childbirth.

As a professional woman with a strong career bias, I would want to argue the case for women recognizing that motherhood is a calling which requires sacrifice, and that babies are born with a need for love which a mother-substitute cannot adequately supply. I have seen the strain on our family when

I have grabbed so-called freedom, that which proves to be no more than a bondage to a profession and which detracts from the first call, motherhood. I have heard the pain of children who grew up uncertain of their worth because parents were too drained to give them love. I have seen adults emotionally crippled because their parents did not understand what was required of them. And so I find myself in agreement with Maxine Hancock when she says:

> The years when a child is basically entrusted to the care of his mother are the most plastic, most critical, most life-shaping years, not only in reference to his mental but also his spiritual and physical development.... If you choose to be a mother, you temporarily, at least, agree to lay aside some of your other involvements, recognizing that bringing children into the world obligates you for their best possible care. The woman who cannot face making her personal interest secondary to the concerns of a family should not have children.[3]

During their formative years children need time, cherishing and love. When they begin school, they especially need mother's availability when they arrive home bursting with excitement or burdened with anxiety.

But surely wives can return to work when the children are older? Isn't this our *right?*

It might be, but in these days of high unemployment we need to ask whether a two-salaried family *is* right. Perhaps we should take up *voluntary* work. Are the children's needs for satisfying relationships being met? If they are not, our off-spring will look elsewhere for love, support and guidance.

I am not saying that it is *never* right for a wife to return to paid employment. I am suggesting that married women should view motherhood as their first responsibility, that they should seek God's guidance about involvement outside the home and that they should beware of being pressurized by society, selfishness or money. It is far better to assume a lower standard of living, and maintain loving relationships within the home, than to place unnecessary strain on everyone because the mother holds down two full-time jobs.

What about the father? Unfortunately there is still current an impression that children are the mother's concern and the father will have no part in their upbringing until they can play football or make him cups of tea. In fact some fathers seem to withdraw from the family when children appear.

A friend of mine, who is a father, feels that this withdrawal is probably a reaction to all the attention the new baby receives. He feels unwanted. His wife has a new centre for her attention. Where *he* was before. All right then, let them do without me, if they don't need me any more! This is a time of difficult readjustment for the father and he needs just as much help as the mother in understanding the new situation.

The Christian husband, however, who is called to give himself to his wife with the love that Christ had, cannot withdraw in this petulant manner. His task is to give his wife the cherishing she still needs, to take turns at waking in the night, to get his hands dirty, literally (is nappy-changing only for women?) and to spend *time* with the child.

Some years ago our car overturned in Yugoslavia, giving me a week in hospital. Only one person spoke English, a doctor. He seemed puzzled by my reply to his question, 'What do you do?' When I insisted, 'I am a wife and mother' he protested that I must have made a mistake; 'It is not enough.' I have tried to show that in one sense he was right, for marriage and family life is not based on a love which focuses inwards, but which reaches out to the world for whom Christ died. But there is a sense in which he was quite wrong. Parenthood is a vocation. Both partners must pool all their resources and lay themselves at the disposal of God for the children He gives them. Parenthood is about making new persons.

Notes for chapter eight

1. D. H. Lawrence, 'Wedlock'.
2. Howard and Charlotte Clinebell, *The Intimate Marriage* (Harper and Row, 1970), p.207.
3. Maxine Hancock, *Love, Honour and be Free* (Pickering and Inglis, 1975), p.88.

9 Sex: The Good News

Sexual intimacy within marriage is a celebration. It is awesome, 'He has taken me to his banquet hall, and the banner he raises over me is love.' It is satisfying, 'In his longed-for shade I am seated and his fruit is sweet to my taste.' And it generates a feeling of belonging, 'I am my beloved's and he is mine' (see Song of Solomon 2 JB).

This good news about sex is promoted, not by a sex-saturated society which would reduce sexual intimacy to a mere plaything, but by the writers of the Bible. The Bible persuades us to believe that the fusion of bodies between husband and wife is not only wholesome, it is born of God. What God creates is good. And sex is good.

God's intention

This word 'good' punctuates the paragraphs of the creation narrative. It describes the whole planet earth. And it is the pithy assessment of the artistry of God after He had made man and woman. As David Mace puts it, 'When the creator had finished his handiwork, he was not assailed with doubts about the wisdom of what he had done. He looked at his creation and congratulated himself that it was a noble effort. He saw that everything he had made – including the maleness and femaleness of the beings created in his own image – was "very good".'[1]

The people whom God created were sexual beings. Their masculinity or femininity was distinguishable by the sex organs which God had designed. This design was perfectly planned so that they would fit into one another. God intended that two into one would go. These beings produced by God came genitally equipped for the love-language of sexual intercourse. The first couple joined their bodies and became 'one flesh'. But they did not blush. They were naked in each other's presence. But they were not ashamed.

Why is it then that Christian couples today turn the good news about sex into bad news? Why do we blush? Why do we squirm? What is it that blocks the road to zestful sexual relationships for some Christian couples? Is this how God intended it to be?

The distortion of sex was never God's intention. Bible writers are uninhibited in their references to sexual intimacy. But the climate changed in the post-apostolic age. It was then that the joys of marital intercourse were dampened by the disdain of church teachers. Take this saying of St Ambrose, for example: 'Married people ought to blush when they consider the sort of life they lead.'

Married people *did* blush. They were embarrassed because they were confused about the purpose of sexual intercourse. Whereas the Bible makes it plain that the sex act has a dual purpose, unitive and procreative, St Augustine, for one, taught that intercourse was sinful unless procreation was the expressed intention. How could someone of the calibre of St Augustine make such a grotesque claim? How could he imply that on one day the sex act is permissible but on another day it is dirty, lustful and profane? As God reminded Peter, 'What God has made clean, you have no right to call profane' (Acts 10:15 JB).

Unfortunately this bad news about sex was not silenced. It was fostered. Christian teachers have been slow to dispel the falsehood that Christian couples should be embarrassed by their sexual activity. The result is that Victorian prudery was piled on medieval monastic shortsightedness. Christian married people feel boxed-in.

Some boxed-in Christians rebuked my husband recently for preaching on the joys of sex in marriage. They accused him of presenting them with a substandard of sanctification. They had been taught that holiness necessitated abstention from sexual intercourse even within marriage. This view is not rare. But it is unbiblical. As Paul reminds the Christians in Corinth, responding to one another sexually is part of the package-deal of marriage. As Lewis Smedes put it, 'When two people get married, each contracts to grant his/her partner the *right* to sexual intercourse....And something is wrong, morally, when married people get into moods that curtail the rights of their partners.'[2]

Something is not only wrong morally, something is wrong spiritually when two people fail to remove the restrictions which erroneous teaching about sex constructs. Some teachers claim that the celibate life is superior to marriage. This teaching is harmful and unbiblical. The Bible clearly presents two possible vocations: the single state and marriage. One is not better than the other. They are different. And both are used in the economy of God to extend His Kingdom.

The confusion about the wholesomeness of sex sometimes stems from the idea that sex is a goddess to be worshipped. Christian couples know, of course, that this is not true. 'You shall have no other gods before me,' says the Lord (Ex. 20:3). But we must not use our reaction against sex worship as an excuse to devalue it. The answer to permissiveness and promiscuity is not no sex but healthy sex. C. S. Lewis expresses beautifully the balance of different kinds of love:

> If God were a substitute for love we ought to have lost all interest in Him. Who'd bother about substitutes when he has the thing itself? But that isn't what happens. We both knew we wanted something...a quite different kind of want. You might as well say that when lovers have one another they will never want to read or eat – or breathe.[3]

Intercourse is therapy

Two married Christian people want God's love, and they want sexual love. They want it because God desires it for them, it signifies far more than the uniting of two physical bodies. This is clearly implied by Paul when he writes that if a Christian resorts to a prostitute he becomes united with her, using the words which God spoke concerning marriage, 'one flesh' (1 Cor. 6:16). If this is so in a 'casual' relationship, how much more is it so in the growing love of marriage? The observation of modern writers often coincides with this biblical attitude. Howard and Charlotte Clinebell express it well when they speak of intercourse as

> ...one of those good bridging experiences! Not only is it a deliciously beautiful way of expressing emotional connectedness, it is a powerful means of strengthening a relationship. Sex feeds love and is fed by love. Everyone at times belongs to the 'walled-off people', to use Dostoyevski's phrase. The physical-emotional-spiritual joining of sex in marriage is a remarkable means of overcoming the walls and of merging two inner worlds. The joining of bodies and spirits is a powerful therapy for our loneliness and inner isolation.[4]

Intercourse is therapy. It completes persons, consoles them and unites them to one another. The Bible suggests that this is one of the purposes of sexual intimacy. 'And Isaac led Rebekah into his tent and made her his wife; and he loved her. And so Isaac was consoled for the loss of his mother' (Gn. 24:67 JB). It is as Jack Dominian says, 'When self esteem is low and confidence lacking the sexual act becomes more than a reassurance, it becomes an urgent therapy, perhaps one of the most powerful forms of treatment the spouses can carry out for one another.'[5]

This therapeutic dimension of sexual intercourse remains a mystery. 'There are three things beyond my comprehension, four, indeed, that I do not understand: the way of an eagle through the skies, the way of a snake over the rocks, the way of a ship in mid-ocean, the way of a man with a girl' (Pr. 30:19 JB). These are things which bring amazement to the writer of Proverbs. No less is the sexual dimension to marriage a great mystery, a source of awe and great wonder.

The writer of the Song of Solomon pinpoints this wonder in the intimacies a man and his bride enjoyed. The book is an explicit love song. He speaks of the delights of sexuality (1:2) and the contentment, satisfaction and peace which it brings (*e.g.* 2:3; 8:10). There is no sense of shame in this poem, only of ecstasy, joy and the pain of separation when the loved one is absent. Intimacy is liberating. It is playful. It is love's creativity which is wholly good.

Was it because Jesus so recognized the importance and joy of intercourse that He reiterated God's first command to couples? The divine injunction is not just to leave parents and cleave to each other. It includes the physical act of becoming 'one flesh'.

Since the Bible presents the joys of intimacy with such enthusiasm and directness, I suggest that, before you read on, you consider the following questions:

Do I bring known sexual hang-ups to our marriage?

Has my religious upbringing been unbiblical or antisexual?

Do I feel it appropriate that as man and wife we should enjoy intercourse, or do I know that fact in my head but reject it with my emotions?

What are my expectations for the sexual aspect of our marriage?

A language to be learned

Is there such a thing as *working* at sex? I believe there is. I reject the popular theory that sex is 'doing what comes naturally'. That may be true of animals. But we are concerned, not with the mere releasing of tension but with a means of communication in which each partner seeks to give pleasure to the other. A few couples are instinctively sensitive and skilful. Most find that sex is a language to be learned. Some learn quickly. Others take years to learn to satisfy each other. Methods of learning vary.

This is not the place for a 'teach yourself guide to sexual intimacy'. A complete ABC of sexual intercourse would, in fact, be harmful because no two married couples are exactly alike. A technique which brings enjoyment to one couple hinders the mutual satisfaction of others. There is absolutely no 'right way' to achieve mutual sexual satisfaction. I am not suggesting that you never refer to a good sex manual.[6] I am saying that an essential pre-requisite for successful sex in marriage is finding the methods which give both of you contentment, happiness and peace. It is the approach which recreates for you that assurance that, through the body, you are no longer two, but one.

74

The starting-point is love, the genuine desire you each have for the well-being of the other. No amount of learning technique, no amount of hard work, will make up for a lack of self-giving. And this applies equally to husbands as to wives. Too long have husbands believed that their wives should sacrifice their feelings and emotions to the whim of the male who needs to be satisfied. Real love is expressed by *both* partners. It is not a one way traffic.

Then remember that there is plenty of time for you to discover your unique pathway to mutually satisfying intercourse. The whole of your future lies before you. You can relax. Relaxation exorcises the tension and anxiety which are the enemies of spontaneous sex. It frees you to laugh when you don't get it right first time.

This is important because humour features largely in the lives of couples who do enjoy carefree sex. It is laughter that turns hurtful experiences into carefree ones. It is humour which says, 'Let's try again, another way.'

To 'try it another way' assumes that you are aware of the variety of patterns for successful love-making. Take the variety of positions, for example. During love-making, the wife might lie on her back with her husband above her. But this might not be the best method for you. Some couples find it preferable to lie side by side facing one another, lying in each other's arms. On the other hand, the husband might be below with his wife above and astride him. Experiment with these positions. Find which is best for you. Be aware that the best position will vary from occasion to occasion. And you won't really know which is your favourite position unless you are prepared to tell each other.

Talking about sex
There is nothing wrong in talking to one another about your sexual experiences. On the contrary, talking about sexual intimacy can help to turn painful experiences into loving ones. Sex, for many couples, is one of their favourite topics of conversation, the subject of many private jokes, the source of wholesome laughter.

This ability to bring sex into the open by talking about it

allays many fears. I think of a girl, Sue, who came to me for help because she was troubled about the question of the frequency of sex. Her mother had given her the impression that *happily* married couples enjoyed intercourse every night. When a whole week passed by and neither Sue nor her husband had felt in the mood for intercourse, she panicked. Was their otherwise happy marriage crumbling? Of course not. But Sue is not the only person worried about frequency. The fact of the matter is that Sue's mother was wrong. Some couples do have intercourse every night, or even oftener. But many couples would find this excessive. Sex would become stale. They prefer to 'make love' once or twice a week. Others sometimes choose to go a whole month without having intercourse. They prefer not to be tied down by someone else's expectations but to be free to adjust to one another's needs and sexual requirements. And they are right.

Sue's mother was not only wrong about frequency. Her advice was also unhelpful in implying that intercourse has to take place at night. Many couples enjoy lazy, leisurely love-making when an uncluttered Saturday morning gives time for the luxury of a 'lie-in'. Others make love at the beginning of an evening when both arrive home from work. It is their way of expressing that they are glad to be united again after the separation of the day. But if this formed the pattern of every evening they might both become bored and the sex act unprofitable.

Just as there is no set time, place or pattern for enjoying sex in marriage, so there is no 'right mood' for ensuring its success. Some couples try to fabricate an aura of passion and romance when, in fact, they are in a playful mood. Playfulness and humour result in frolicsome sex. This is not less authentic than the kind of intimacy which is urgent, passionate and erotic. It is different. And the gentle, relaxed, lazy feelings which lead to leisurely love-making help us to understand that sexual intercourse is not a performance governed by strict rules and regulations. Rather it is a delicate art-form requiring sensitivity, understanding and freedom of expression.

The artistic expression of love embraces, not only the moment of climax, when both partners experience that 'good-all-over' feeling of contentment and peace, but also the vital moments of fore-play which precede the act of intercourse. The purpose of this love-play needs to be understood. There is no virtue in keeping silence when a sensitive lifting of the veil would help married people to adjust to one another, to understand the other and to enjoy sexual love-play.

This fore-play which leads to intercourse is improved by skin to skin closeness. Nakedness is therefore an aid to intimacy. When married people have removed their clothing it is easy and natural to slip into the tenderness which is so important for the wife. Unlike her husband, she might not be aroused quickly. Her excitement will increase and intensify as her husband gently fondles her breasts or strokes her thighs. Gentleness and patience are essential. You should never be in a hurry. Even though the man's penis has enlarged and he is sexually aware and excited, his wife may not be ready for intercourse. It usually takes longer for the vagina to be completely lubricated and the wife is not ready for penetration until that lubrication is complete. Haste, impatience and impetuous behaviour are not loving and can result in emotional, even physical, pain.

Sexual nerve-endings are located in the penis, making it a very sensitive organ when enlarged. The most sensitive zone in the woman is the clitoris. It is the key to bringing the wife to orgasm. The rhythmical movement of the clitoris in response to the movement of the penis produces the exciting sensations which lead to climax. This climax is followed by feelings of well-being, achievement and peace. It is love resting.

Newly married people frequently fail to experience this delicious rest because they are nervous, clumsy and rough. These barriers to enjoyable sex need not last. But it is intelligent understanding and loving consideration of one another, not silence, which removes obstacles.

As a married couple you might therefore find it helpful to respond to these questions:

What kind of sexual fore-play gives me most pleasure?
What kinds of touch do I most enjoy?
What emotional benefits do I receive from the sexual side of our marriage?

Do I feel there is anything we need to work at?

The good news about sex in marriage is that it is the consummation of the marital relationship which God designed. It is the mysterious way in which two individuals become one flesh. The secret of successful sex in marriage, where you discover that sex *is* good, is the willingness to work at it. This is a joyful task. It enables you to discover, in a gradual way, a method and a programme which is unique to the two of you. It shows you that sex is not so much a performance to be practised as a series of experiences to be enjoyed.

Notes for chapter nine

1. David R. Mace, *The Christian Response to the Sexual Revolution* (Lutterworth, 1971), p.15.
2. Lewis Smedes, *Sex in a Real World* (Lion, 1979), pp.222 f.
3. C. S. Lewis, *A Grief Observed* (Faber, 1961), p.10.
4. Howard and Charlotte Clinebell, *The Intimate Marriage* (Harper and Row, 1970), p.137.
5. Jack Dominian, *Marital Breakdown* (Pelican, 1971), p.81.
6. Maxine Davis, *Sexual Responsibility in Marriage* (Fontana, 1977), is to be recommended, though not written from a Christian point of view.
   Ed and Gaye Wheat, *Intended for Pleasure* (Scripture Union, 1979), is a useful, if basic, treatment written by Christians.

10 Meeting Sexual Problems

In the last chapter we examined the claim that for two Christian married people the sexual act is a love language expressing emotional, physical and spiritual oneness. We emphasized that getting off to a slow start sexually does not necessarily condemn a couple to a life of sexual incompatibility

Many couples, however, find that there are occasions in marriage when their sexual relating does not go well. There seems to be a conspiracy of silence veiling this fact, which contributes to feelings of inadequacy and the fear that the marriage might disintegrate. A double bed then becomes a very lonely place.

The fact of the matter is that there is a rhythm about sexual desire, not only for a woman with her monthly period, but for her husband as well. The menstrual cycle affects a woman's potential for sexual arousal. Most women experience maximal sexual desire immediately before or after menstruation, while their desire for sex and potential for quick arousal are low during the middle of their monthly cycle. And men also experience a slump in desire as well as a peak but for reasons which are less apparent.

The slump in sexual interest in men (and women) often coincides with over-tiredness, stress and anxiety. Successful intercourse depends not only on the depth of love a couple have for one another, but also on their physical well-being, their psychological peace of mind and their emotional and spiritual health. So a relaxed evening together, a weekend away or paying careful attention to practical, even mundane ways of keeping love alive in marriage, often provide a solution for flagging sexual desire.

When you experience a sexual low, before leaping to the conclusion that your sex life is irreparable, check the following:

Is there a pattern which could indicate your personal rhythm?

Are you, or your partner, under stress at work, at church or in the family?

Are you out of sorts with one another?

Are you perhaps wanting to punish your partner for something he/she is failing to do or be?

Have you made time to relax together recently?

What are you hoping for from your sexual relationship?

Expectations

I included the last question because sometimes the reasons for sexual ineptitude are not obvious. Take the confusion caused by the over-glamourization of sex for example. Glossy magazines, films and books tell us how we *ought* to enjoy intercourse. They spare no details. The technique is traced step by step. Sometimes, as in a good sex manual, the aim is wholesome. But the danger is that sex then becomes performance-centred rather than love-centred. Couples come to marriage with romantic expectations of the daily, passionate, exotic jaunts which sex will provide. But when they discover that sex is sometimes gentle, sometimes mundane and sometimes almost non-existent, they feel cheated and angry.

Real sex in real life is not so much a performance, what you do, as a method of communication, what you are attempting to say. Sexual intimacy, therefore, is not a test which you pass or fail. There is no 'right way' of doing it. Rather, it is the attempt one couple makes to express love to one another and in some ways the method will be unique to each separate couple. No experience of intimacy which originates from mutual desire to express love is wasted, however fumbling it may appear to be. One or both of you may fail to reach a climax, that 'good-all-over' feeling, but that does not cancel out the fun of genital fore-play or the contentment of lying in your partner's arms. Sexual intercourse is an offering of your whole self to the one you love.

When Geoff and Val talked to me they had not grasped this.

They had learned that sex is a series of thrills to be experienced, something to be grabbed, not something to be given. Intercourse therefore became the respository for all the doubts and fears about sex which each had brought to the marriage. Geoff feared that he would never be able to satisfy Val. Val felt, deep down, that 'nice' girls didn't enjoy sex. So every magazine they read on the subject seemed to confirm their dread that, sexually, they were inadequate and incompetent.

Since they had also absorbed another erroneous claim that sex is the axis on which healthy marriages turn, Geoff and Val felt that they were in serious marital trouble. Let Jack Dominian, Director of the Marital Research Centre in London, put sex in its right perspective:

> In clinical experience there is ample evidence to suggest that sexual orgasm is neither essential for sexual relief nor is its absence an inevitable contribution to marital breakdown. Sexual intercourse itself may be completely absent and a marriage remain happy. This is not to underrate the importance of the physical exchange in marriage but to emphasize that successful orgastic experience is not an essential pre-requisite for marital happiness. One eminent worker has summarized succinctly the situation: 'It is necessary to make it clear from the start that an orgasm is not a panacea for all marital woe...I have never seen a marriage made or broken by sex alone, except in the case of frank perversions.'[1]

For couples like Geoff and Val, a change of attitude is required. It comes with the realization of the truth about sex, that 'penises and vaginas do not make love. They only do what complete human beings tell them to do...*sexual intercourse is not what you do: sexual intercourse is who you are.*'[2]

Failure to understand these facts puts a couple under severe pressure when they have to abstain from intercourse in the later stages of pregnancy or during times of illness.

Illness sometimes saps all strength and desire for physical contact. When a person has had an operation, for example, he may be too exhausted to think about sex. Pain and fear of pain make body-closeness intolerable. If couples believe that sex is the be-all and end-all of marriage, these times become periods of great frustration and anger. The truth is that almost always the return of strength and vitality is accompanied by the awakening of the longing for intercourse. In the period of waiting, which may last for months, it is esential to be patient with one another and to recognize that a vital part of married life is just jogging along, even struggling along, supporting each other. If you are both going through such a stage, tell your partner your reaction to these questions:

How am I feeling about our relationship at the moment?

How do I feel about the way we are coping with our problems?

If a couple have been forced to abstain from intercourse for a prolonged period, they may find it difficult to come back together again. It happened to us on one occasion. I slipped a disc playing badminton and a few months later sustained back injuries in a car crash. The two accidents meant that for over a year we were unable to have intercourse. When my back was better, I wanted to enjoy sex again but I was afraid of the pain which it might cause. The fear made me tense and unresponsive. Eventually, we discovered for ourselves the value of taking our sexual problem to someone who knew how to help us. This person allowed us to talk and then, sensing my fear, simply asked God to release me from the bondage in which fear held me and to restore to us the gift of marital sex. Having experienced the value of counselling and the ministry of prayer for ourselves we have no hesitation in recommending it to you if you find yourselves experiencing sexual problems.

Reasons for seeking help

Just as illness prompts a visit to the doctor, so sexual 'ailments' should push a couple into seeking specialized advice. There are several reasons why you should seek help *together*. First, you have a great need to understand one another's feelings during times of sexual dissatisfaction.

There is the need to understand the negative message which refusing to respond sexually conveys. This ultimate refusal of husband or wife to respond sexually communicates maximum rejection to your partner. Jack Dominian draws our attention to the positive message sexual intercourse conveys:

> One of the principal features of the act…is the powerful reassurance it gives to couples at *all* times but particularly during special periods of need, that each wants and is prepared to accept the other undconditionally. This is an unconditional acceptance which is not in evidence elsewhere in life, except in the early and unspoiled relationship between the baby and its mother.[3]

When this acceptance is lacking and when sexual intimacy is absent or in short supply, it increases the possibility that one or both partners will look beyond the marriage for affection and sexual fulfilment. It aggravates the temptation to fantasize and to masturbate. And this is the second reason for finding a way through sexual problems when they arise. Our aim as Christians should be to turn away from the folly and hollowness of adulterous and sick relationships with the pain that they bring and, in the words of the writer of Proverbs, a man should rejoice constantly in the wife of his youth, being satisfied with *her* breasts and captivated by *her* love (see Pr. 5:18–23).

When rejection is nursed it grows and is translated into anger, aggression and bitterness. Misplaced anger creates a destructive cycle. It is this cycle that brings a couple to the point of breakdown, not sexual dissatisfaction *per se*.

Val felt conned by the whole sex story. Her secret fear was that there was something radically wrong with herself which prevented her enjoying the sex thrills she had read about. But it was too risky to acknowledge her real fears and so she pinned the blame onto Geoff. He didn't take care to arouse her properly, he was 'sex mad', it was all he thought about. She blamed him for other things too: his neglect of herself and the children, his extravagance, the attention lavished on his parents. And Geoff was afraid that it *was* all his fault. But with Val he kept the mask in place and accused her of not caring about him, of not looking after their home, and criticized the way she dressed. In the end, Val punished Geoff by refusing all sexual intimacy. It was this punishment that brought them to the point of recognizing that, unless they sought help, their marriage would disintegrate.

Another motive for hacking a path through the jungle from sexual ineptitude to sexual satisfaction is Paul's reminder to Christians in Corinth that sexual intimacy is your partner's right. Couples should abstain, therefore, only for the purpose of prayer, by mutual agreement and for a limited period. A partner who forces his/her partner into celibacy is sinning against the partner.

Some common problems

Some couples plead that they could not possibly seek help. They are embarrassed, shy, unable to talk about sex. All those reasons are understandable and few people want to talk to a third person about a relationship which is essentially private. But a further reason why you should seek help is that great strides are being made in the ability counsellors have to assist couples. Although you may feel tongue-tied, a counsellor will know how to 'talk sexually' and will not be embarrassed. In most cases couples who ask can be helped to give one another greater sexual satisfaction.

Take *the inability to experience orgasm* for example. Many marriages are disrupted by 'orgasmic failure' and women have told me of the despair they experience when this persists over a prolonged period. Most of the women who have spoken to me think they are alone in their suffering and few hold out any hope of improvement. But both of these assumptions are inaccurate.

Research has revealed some interesting statistics. Kinsey, for example, found that, of the women in his study, 50% had not achieved orgasm during the first month of marriage, 25% had not reached a climax by the end of the first year and 10% continued to experience anorgasmia, as it is called, after fifteen years of marriage. But the assurance that you are not the only one is cold comfort unless it is accompanied by hope for improvement.

And there *is* hope. Many couples are delighting in the sexual side of marriage as a result of the help they have received. The nature of the help available is varied and will, of course, differ from couple to couple. Some couples simply need an understanding third person who will listen, talk

84

through the delicate situation and defuse the tension which has built up. We saw in chapter 3 how therapy of this kind helped Barry and Doreen to resolve their apparent sexual incompatibility.

Other couples require more specialized help, for instance teaching both partners to be more relaxed. It might focus on basic attitudes which prevent one partner from accepting sex as God's gift, something to celebrate and to enjoy. A husband can learn new ways of arousing his wife so that she is as excited about sex as he is. It is generally accepted that women can be helped to reach a climax by stimulation of the clitoris and a man can learn how to help his wife in this way. This learning has been so successful for many couples, that, even if you find such discussions distasteful, it is foolish to ignore the available advice. This talk about 'technique' need not make a nervous bride feel that she is nothing but an instrument to be played on. The emphasis will be, not on sex as performance, but on intercourse as it is meant to be, an expression of mutual love. Help is also available in the form of drugs but these are only available from your doctor and should, of course, be used only when prescribed by him.

Some husbands discover that they are unable to *maintain erection*. It is not clear why some men experience this difficulty but it is more obvious why it causes stress for the wife. Some women seem to enjoy a series of climaxes, rather than one specific short-lived orgasm but the claim is made that most women respond best if the penis remains in the vagina for a period varying from one to eleven minutes. It is these women who are disappointed if their husband is unable to maintain an erection for more than a few seconds.

Talking about the problem might help you to unearth the reasons why the husband is experiencing difficulty. Fatigue or anxiety might be contributing factors. Feelings of guilt, shame, confusion and disappointment can be safely confronted in the presence of a counsellor who will help you to work through them. And wives can be shown ways of applying stimulus to their husbands in an attempt to prolong the periods of erection. These methods may succeed; they may fail. But the understanding and acceptance of one another which you gain by seeking help together is not wasted.

Many couples also need help with the problem of *premature ejaculation*. Some men reach a climax very rapidly, sometimes outside the vagina and often immediately after entering. In the excitement of sexual fore-play, some semen is ejaculated prematurely, and it seems difficult to control the quantity. When everything seems to happen so quickly for her husband, a wife can be left feeling cheated, even insulted by him. Both of you can learn ways of helping each other to achieve greater sexual satisfaction. A husband can be shown how to control the amount of sperm which leaks before entering and his wife can learn ways of helping him.

Some couples approach marriage full of misunderstandings and *unexpressed fears*. Some women are frightened that intercourse will hurt them, afraid of an unwanted pregnancy and many are still ashamed to admit that they want to enjoy sex. Other women fear that they are 'too small' to enjoy sexual intercourse, that the vagina is not large enough to accommodate a penis. And men have similar fears. I think of several men who have expressed their uncertainty about their ability to satisfy a woman because they fear they are too small. Ribald remarks made in changing rooms and graffiti on the walls of men's toilets seem to confirm these fears. Others are afraid they are too big. I always admire people who have the courage to voice such fears. It seems that at last the myth has been exploded by the findings of Masters and Johnson who claim, on the basis of their research, that, 'Almost any vagina can stretch to accommodate any penis and the size of the penis or clitoris has no correlation with the degree of sexual pleasure attained.'[4]

Fantasies

In this chapter I have emphasized the need couples have to seek advice together. The reason is because the correlation between the sexual and all other aspects of the marriage is very close. Few find sustained closeness with another easy. This is why some people opt into the world of erotic fantasy which seems to offer the attractions of love devoid of demand. The fact that this is the antithesis of love which takes as its model the 'God who so loved that He gave', eludes them at such moments. They are conscious only of a compelling desire and they allow yearnings to master them rather than allowing the all-conquering Christ to control their desires.

Stephen had just this problem and its roots reached right back to his childhood. His mother had a great need to be loved by him and made many demands and Stephen instinctively longed to receive love with no strings attached. Although she was demanding, his mother did not give him what he really needed. There was never any mention of sex at home, for example, and if ever the word was mentioned on the radio, Stephen gained the impression that somehow it wasn't 'nice'. Yet all the boys at school bragged about the information they had gleaned and, since he was the gang's ring-leader, he would make up stories, even tell them his version of how the sex act was performed. And they believed him. But how they would mock and despise him if they knew how little information he really had. Stephen's world of fantasy had been brought into being.

By the time he was in his teens, Stephen found himself turning to girly magazines, trying to prove his masculinity to himself with the erotic thrills they afforded. He still possessed very few facts about sex, but sexual fantasy was becoming an obsession. The problem gradually became too big for him. He seemed unable now to stop looking at women lustfully. He couldn't turn his eyes away from posters and deliberately thumbed through pornographic magazines. When he became a Christian, he wanted to stop. He suspected that his fantasy world was included in Jesus' teaching about adultery.

He couldn't bear the thought of persistently failing God so he pushed these spiritual thoughts away.

And then he fell in love with Marion. When they were married, it would be different. He wouldn't need to turn love in on himself. She would love him and not make demands. But he found that marriage, too, is a costly form of loving. And he still took the pile of magazines from the cupboard.

Stephen's obsession was born in childhood from experiences which were out of his control. The past often contains the roots of insecurity, lack of self-worth and the inability to accept ourselves. Painful memories which are stored away retain a hold over the present. This is frightening when it is recognized that the way two people relate sexually in marriage is partly governed by the past. But there is hope, hope for the girl who has experienced the horrors of rape, for those who have lived promiscuously, for those who have suffered as a result of parental unfaithfulness. And there was hope for Stephen. Christ is greater than our past. He is able to remove the sting from past memories so that they lose their hold on a person in bondage. When God said, 'If the Son shall set you free you shall be free indeed', it included freedom from the effects of your own past as well as forgiveness for your guilt.

When Stephen and Marion realized this they asked for the ministry of prayer. Stephen came clean with God and Marion for the first time. He produced all the skeletons from the cupboard and allowed the light of Christ to shine on them. It was then that he knew that he was forgiven by God and Marion in unconditional love. When he heard Marion tell him that she still loved him he wept. All the years of searching in magazines and the unknown faces of girls in the subway had failed to bring this assurance. Stephen knew that he was free. Not free in the sense that he would never be tempted again. He is, after all, a real flesh and blood man. But free from the obsession. The tap-root was removed.

Jesus said, 'Ask and you will receive.'
Are there known sexual problems spoiling your marriage?
Are there problems which are still hidden from your partner?
Are there areas which need God's and each other's forgiveness?
How do you feel about seeking help together?
Do you believe that through the ministry of prayer you can be set free?

Notes for chapter ten

1. Jack Dominian, *Marital Breakdown* (Pelican, 1971), p.78.
2. Urban G. Steinmetz, *I Will* (Ave Maria Press, 1978), p.97.
3. Jack Dominian, *op.cit.*, p.80.
4. Quoted by Howard and Charlotte Clinebell, *The Intimate Marriage* (Harper and Row, 1970), p.152.

11 Tension: Gateway to Strength

Something happened which caused me to discard my careful plan for this chapter. I had all the insights I could find neatly listed. I knew what I wanted to communicate about the place of conflict in healthy marriages. And then, eight days after a very happy holiday together, David and I clashed (as we do from time to time). Conflict invaded our marriage. At first I was disappointed. Then I was just cross. It was like finding spiders playing in your bath when you come home from holiday. But then, I argued, had I not just written words like, 'tension in marriage need not destroy, it can recreate, build, make lovely'? Had I not intended to say that disharmony between partners can be a 'friend in disguise'? We put into practice some of the suggestions I had planned to make, but we remained as much at variance as before.

While we were searching for a way out of our deadlock, I wrote this sentence, 'This thing is too big for me. I cannot handle it.' A few hours later, the word of God, with the incisiveness of the sharp, two-edged sword which it is, thrust its message into the situation: 'My grace is sufficient for you, for my power is made perfect in weakness' (2 Cor. 12:9).

The elusive, missing factor was now so obvious. We had been trying, in our own strength, to make tension work for us so that it became creative and not destructive. But in our own strength we can do nothing. It is while drawing on a power greater than our own, the strength of God, that such miracles take place. This verse reminded me of the truth that when conflict interrupts marital harmony, Christ waits to be invited into the place of tension to convert destructive energies into creative power. I rediscovered that I must neither play God nor imitate Him. Rather, as creature, I must co-operate with Him, allowing Him the privilege and responsibility of being God.

Jesus is the key we had mislaid. But now that I have rediscovered for myself the relevance of Himself, I feel confident to reiterate that conflict in marriage need not destroy. Acknowledged tension, placed into the hands of God, can transform marriage. Tension reveals your complementarity, the 'otherness' which distinguishes you from your partner. It offers opportunities for adjustment and growth. If forms a gateway to intimacy. But this intimacy does not happen instantaneously, as Paul and Brenda found.

Weekdays were hectic for Brenda. She had a full time job and she was new to the area, so shopping seemed to take a long time. Then there was the washing, the ironing and the cleaning of the flat. But she really looked forward to Sundays. After church in the morning she and Paul enjoyed a leisurely lunch and then they would wash up together and settle down for a relaxed afternoon doing a jig-saw puzzle, chatting, simply being lazy. At least that was Brenda's dream of how Sundays should be.

Paul found the week flashed by too. His research project kept him at work most days and several evenings, sometimes late into the night. He sometimes felt guilty that he didn't help Brenda more. But there was Sunday. They would relax over lunch. Then they could shut the kitchen door on the washing-up until tea-time and just enjoy being together. He would take on the kitchen duties on Sunday evening to give Brenda a break.

Gradually Sunday afternoons became a battlegound. You may think that to disagree over something as trivial as washing-up was stupid, but then, conflict often does erupt over trivialities. The washing-up was the tip of an iceberg. It showed Paul that Brenda was 'just like her mum', who always washed up immediately after a meal was finished. And it showed her that he was just like his dad, who would never dream of working on a Sunday afternoon. The story ended happily because they worked through the turbulent stage and reached a compromise. If you go to their house for Sunday lunch, the chances are that at 2.00pm on the dot, they will wash up together. That's the compromise which both are happy with.

During the first year of marriage a couple establishes patterns of behaviour which are not easily changed. But establishing good patterns is not always straightforward for two people who bring to the relationship a variety of tastes, habits and expectations. In considering how you might create healthy patterns, I shall refer frequently to St Paul's ode to love in 1 Corinthians 13 and Paul and Brenda's experience, using them as a work basis.

The key: the love of Jesus
Paul and Brenda soon discovered that if you keep the lid on a boiling pan, the contents spill over. They found that the Sunday afternoon problem sparked off irritability. They were waspish towards each other about nothing and everything until they took the lid off their emotions and allowed the anger to cool down.

Then they learned to be real with one another. They realized that it was pointless to pretend that the problem was not there. That would be as foolish as rolling the carpet over a hole in the floor, hoping that you wouldn't fall through, or that the carpet would make the hole go away. Holes in floorboards grow bigger if left unattended. The same is true of marital tension.

Both were well armed with defensive weapons, as most of us are. Both could boast that his/her plan for Sunday afternoon was superior to the partner's. But boasting is a cover-up for the inner fears which make us suspect that our ideas may not be so good after all. Both were quite capable of arrogance. Arrogant protestations sound convincing but they are really pride camouflaging an inner hollowness.

Both were rude, that rough, ungracious method of communication which rides rough-shod over another, the language used by insecure people who wish to boost their own ego. Rudeness is a barrier to intimacy.

But when Paul and Brenda used these tactics, the warfare intensified. Love, writes St Paul, is not boastful, arrogant or rude. Love makes for a genuine, authentic, self-controlled person.

It was when this young couple faced conflict with the poise which is the fruit of genuineness and authenticity that they began to glimpse a satisfactory solution. Love for one another and their relationship transcended their need to clamour for their own rights. It dismissed resentments, those memories which had been carefully stored and lovingly fingered so that they could be reintroduced at strategic moments. Because they loved one another, Paul and his wife realized that they could not afford play-acting. They had to learn to express to one another what was really going on inside each of them.

When they did this they began to realize that tension is a referee's whistle, signalling the opportunity to go off the field, evaluate objectively what has happened and come back for the second half with the team reunited. Then hope is revived. In marriage, hope is expressed in determination to overcome and willingness to try life another way. To love is to hope: and hope keeps love alive.

Paul and Brenda are not the sort of people who find it easy to unveil their feelings, but they tried. Like others before them, ordinary young people, or eminent persons like Dag Hammarskjöld and Catherine Marshall, they decided to record their feelings by writing them down. As they did so, they saw the importance of clarification. Then emotions heated in the crucible of solitude lose their perspective. When they are revealed and exposed to the loving gaze of another, the dross can be discarded and the precious metal retained.

I was glad that these young friends of mine could tell their story with a sense of humour. Humour and honesty help us to face conflict. I also appreciated the way they determined that they would be in the situation together; *they were for each other, not against each other.*

Their attitude reminds me of what St Paul writes about love, the love which is patient with another and which suffers that which irritates and annoys, for a very long time. Long-suffering leads to reconciliation; it facilitates Christ's healing and grants Him permission to remove the tap-root of sin which is so often the origin of conflict.

The way Paul and Brenda reached a happy compromise reminds me, too, of St Paul's phrase, 'love is kind'. Kindness is that tough, unromantic compassison which accurately assesses another's need and which compels us to act appropriately for that person. Kindness is not a sloppy, sentimental attempt to perpetuate romantic love; it is acting at cost to yourself. It is the clear-headed compassion of a Florence Nightingale, the unstinted availability of a Mother Teresa of Calcutta, supremely, the sacrifical involvement of Jesus Christ.

I am not suggesting that Paul and Brenda never argued again. I suspect that they are sometimes irritable with one another, as most couples are; but their conflict has much to teach us about the way to handle disagreement. It shows the importance of being real with one another, of providing a safe place where you may each ventilate negative feelings. It points out that the opposites of love – boasting, arrogance, rudeness – are counter-productive and need to be replaced by self-control, careful, objective evaluation and the willingness to try life another way. It emphasizes the attitude that 'we're in it together' and the importance of the kind of love which St Paul describes, the Christian love which produces more love. This cements relationships and heals them.

This love, which St Paul describes, did not have its source in Paul or Brenda. Without the love of Jesus they would still have walked round each other in suspicion and resentment. Only when they saw themselves in the light of Jesus did they see how self-centred they had become. Once again, Jesus is the key.

Whether a couple makes a success or failure of marriage depends partly on their attitude to conflict. We look at some danger signals in this chapter and consider specific problem areas in the next.

Some dangers to avoid
David and Vera Mace divide couples into three categories. They speak of *conflict-excluding, conflict-avoiding* and *conflict-resolving* couples.[1]

The first picture illustrates what happens when the Bible's

1. *Conflict-excluding* 2. *Conflict-avoiding* 3. *Conflict-resolving*

teaching about submission is misunderstood or misappropriated. The couple adopt, to borrow the Maces' phrase, a one-vote system, in which the husband assumes total authority and in which the wife's opinion is considered to be of little worth. The thick line between them indicates the blockage to intimacy which this attitude erects.

The second picture looks more hopeful, but careful observation shows that, though husband and wife are seen to be equals, there is a new barrier to closeness. The barrier is there because, although each recognizes the other's worth, when conflict arises between them, they pretend it is not there. The conflict-avoiding attitude encourages the fear that there are certain subjects which a couple dare not discuss because on previous occasions confrontation led to the sort of tension which neither of them can tolerate.

We have already seen that conflict-resolving couples discover new and sometimes amusing pathways through conflict by making disagreement work for them. Paul and Brenda looked like the third couple when they talked to me. The danger of avoiding conflict is that you distance one another. Some couples have spoken to me of the coldness in their relationship which led to literal, spatial distancing where the couples sleep in separate rooms. Others described the psychological separateness whereby you stop communicating verbally, you roll over and turn your back on one another in bed, you isolate your partner from your real self. This kind of non-relating leads to insomnia and depression. Just as love produces love, so coldness produces frigidity.

There are more dangers: 'dirty fighting', 'game playing', 'putting one another down' and playing 'tit-for-tat'. They are the methods conflict-avoiding couples use to relate over the fences which separate them.

'Dirty fighting' is when you both harbour resentments against each other. Each misdemeanour is tucked away in your memory like a favourite stowaway whom you visit from time to time, gaining sick comfort from the experience relived. Then by reminding the other of the way he/she failed you yesterday, last week, last year, you attempt to undermine his/her self-esteem. Most couples enjoy 'dirty fighting' from time to time but it is not Christlike living. It barricades the entrance to forgiveness, acceptance and understanding. Dirty fighting can be replaced by 'clean fighting' which is the ability to deal with mutual resentments openly with the frank recognition that you both have weaknesses, both fail and both need the covering of the forgiving love of Christ. This kind of 'fighting' restores appreciation, affection and respect, and does not then continue after peace is restored.

'Game playing' is that system couples use to relate with one another in a mutually manipulative manner. Communication is never straightforward. There is always an ulterior motive. It leads to 'tit-for-tat' relating whereby a husband supports his wife one evening so that he can demand 'mothering' the next. Or a wife smiles sweetly as her husband departs for the prayer meeting on Monday because that gives her the right to use the car on Wednesday.

'Putting one another down' is employed by couples who are both insecure or who need to compete with their partner in the company of others. Whenever an opportunity arises, they delight in interrupting when the partner is speaking, contradicting to give a good impression or disagreeing for the sake of winning an argument.

When these bad patterns are established, one of two things

might happen to the conflict-avoiding couple. They might construct a congenial, frictionless, distant relationship with the occasional flicker of the diseased relating I have described. Or scrapping might become a way of life. I recall one couple who came to see me, shrieking at each other. They paused only for a quick aside to me, 'Don't worry about us, it's always like this.' They had grown accustomed to their frequent flare-ups but I wondered if they realized how much unintentional hurt resulted from the flying sparks.

There is however, a place for hostility in marriage. Negative feelings can make a valuable contribution to a relationship. Take jealousy for example. It can gnaw at love like a cancerous growth but it can also demonstrate how much you love one another. It depends how you look at it and what you do with the desire to possess. It partly depends on your willingness to allow love (and God is love) to convert negative emotions into positive ones.

The difference between intimacy and superficiality is that when people are close they tell one another how they are, how they feel, what constitutes the real 'me'. In shallow relationships, persons relate only on the level of what they do, what they think and what is happening in their world. Those who choose a hollow, empty kind of relating find that conflict adds to the experience of emptiness. But those who are prepared for the hard work which closeness involves, discover that tension can be a friend in disguise.

How can you apply this truth to your marriage?
When tension arises will you ask yourself three questions:
What does this situation teach me about myself?
What does it show me about my partner?
What does it reveal about our relationship?

Notes for chapter eleven

1. David and Vera Mace, *We can have better marriages if we want them* (Oliphants, no date), p.84.

12 The Power of Creative Love

Marriage is like the little girl in the nursery rhyme. When it is good, it is very, very good. But when it is bad it is horrid.

Tension in marriage can be creative. But conflict can be as irritating to a relationship as wasps buzzing round your marmalade at breakfast. Trouble, therefore, requires firm and authoritative handling. In this chapter, we will broaden our understanding of marital conflict by considering some of its causes.

Some causes of marital disharmony
One major reason for tense feelings experienced by some couples during the early months of marriage is the loneliness which is created by the sense of displacement some people suffer whenever changes take place. Like plants, some people show a remarkable capacity to adapt to new surroundings. Others have fewer powers of adaptation and any major change in their lives produces lethargy, a kind of wilting and even panic. Displacement, even by that which is good, can feel threatening until it is replaced by a new routine.

Take Will and Anna, for example. Their marriage relationship is described in a novel and provides a useful base from which to observe the crises of early marriage.

They planned their honeymoon in an idyllic cottage in the country, from which the outside world would be excluded. Those days together were bliss. Will let Anna do what she liked with him. Her undivided attention and personal love provided him with unfamiliar feelings of security and well-being. He became like a contented child. The fact that he displayed all the signs of the exaggerated dependence of childhood didn't seem to matter. Anna was there just for him; he became obedient and compliant to her every whim.

For a while, Anna, too, revelled in the delights of love and the cottage was filled with the sound of her joyful, tinkling laughter. She was so happy with marriage that she wanted to share their joy with others. So she opened the cottage door and invited her friends in, whereupon Will slumped like a spoilt child. He felt abandoned. And since Anna had hurt him he retaliated.

The author makes this comment on the infant marriage: 'One day it seemed as if everything was shattered, all life spoiled, ruined, desolated and laid waste. The next day it was all marvellous again, just marvellous. One day she thought she would go mad from his very presence... the next day she loved and rejoiced in the way he crossed the floor, he was sun, moon and stars in one.'[1]

There is nothing wrong with two adults relating to one another occasionally as if they were children. Lovers may find a 'pet' name for one another, talk baby-love to one another, run with the wind, just like children do. The problem is that when one or both are unable to revert to adulthood, an imbalance is created. Adults are people who make responsible choices, seek to understand others, and work for the personal good of another. But this Will and Anna could not do, and their immaturity triggered off a series of crises: a dependency crisis, an intimacy crisis and an 'otherness' crisis. We look at these in detail. They are the stuff of which marital conflict is made.

Dependency

A dependency crisis arises when one partner's emotional needs push him/her into making unreasonable demands on the spouse. When a wife expects her husband to be to her all that her father was at his best, and to compensate for all her father failed to give her, marital storms brew. When a husband's needs demand that his wife should be to him mother, mistress, companion and colleague all of the time, an undercurrent of tension will continuously disturb marital harmony. Many people unconsciously make these unreasonable demands. They have not yet reached emotional maturity, usually for very good reasons.

The problem is perpetuated when one's partner inevitably fails to come up to expectations. As with Will, the hurt half of the relationship then hits out with the cruelty of a child or the aggressiveness of an adolescent.

Virginia Satir suggests a way out of the downward spiral. She proposes that couples look carefully at one another and listen to one another. Does your partner remind you of anyone? Father, maybe, or uncle? If so, when tension arises, you need to ask whether it is your partner you are relating to or whether you have slipped back in time and emotion to a previous relationship which still has some sort of hold over you. Are you perhaps attempting to *punish* a parent-figure through your spouse?

Another positive step to strengthen your marriage is to recognize the truth about people. The average person is dependable some of the time. The average person is equipped to give support and advice to others on occasions. He is not qualified to be dependable, rock-like, strong, all of the time. There are situations in life which expose the weakness of the strong, which uncover the vulnerability of the well-integrated person and which cause the rock-like to crumble. On such occasions they are the ones who stretch out a desperate hand. They need to be rescued. You may think you have married one of the world's helpers, someone who is always prepared to mount a rescue operation. But, at best, your partner is no more than a wounded healer who will sometimes prop you up and who will, on occasions, require support from you.

Couples who are prepared for both eventualities, those who are generous enough and mature enough to see the need for giving as well as receiving are the ones who will most easily dispel tension. They recognize that they married a real person, not Superman, or Wonder Woman.

Moreover, Christian couples know that there is a place of resourcefulness to which they can always turn. It is to be found in Jesus. He is our safe place, our refuge, the supplier for our deepest needs. With this recognition, we can release our partner from unrealistic demands. We are free to explode the theory that marriage meets our every need. We are at liberty to see the marital relationship and our partner for what they are, one of the vehicles, but only one, which God chooses to use to supply our need for love.

Intimacy

The intimacy crisis confounded Will and Anna. Like many other couples, they discovered that Will's preference for solitude did not match his wife's gregarious personality. All Will wanted was Anna's attention or solitude. But Anna so overflowed with the benefits of love that she needed to share them with others. Will interpreted her need for friends as a rejection of himself. Anna assumed that, like herself, Will also felt a need to draw others into their love. A vicious circle was drawn.

This problem is experienced by many couples, and it is not solved until two discoveries are made. First, a person's privacy must be guarded, the value of solitude respected. Second, some people thrive on friendships but those relationships do not imply rejection of the partner in marriage. They are an expression of the appreciation and enthusiasm which marriage has given them.

When an outgoing wife, like Anna, clashes with her shy husband in this way, the problem will not be solved until they clarify the confused emotions which give rise to wrong assumptions. It will be necessary for each to bear full responsibility for the fears which arise. It will be essential to communicate openly and honestly with one another: 'I feel as if you are rejecting me, as if our marriage doesn't matter as much to you as it does to me. I don't understand your need for other people because I don't share it.' It is vital that, just as the loner must allow the partner freedom to cultivate friendships so the more social partner should exercise sensitivity in choosing friends.

You could avoid this kind of conflict by responding to the following questions:

Which friendships are right for the present?
How much time should be spent nurturing them?
Are our friendships mutually enriching or mutually exclusive?

Which is more difficult for me: to allow you free access to people and activities which enrich you or to give you space from me?

'Otherness'

The 'otherness' crisis occurs when the differences between partners become an occasion for criticism. The problem is resolved when two people recognize that their differences contain all the potential for improving the marriage. Differences do not condemn a marriage to failure. In fact God made us differently so that we could fulfil a variety of functions. Dismay about the 'otherness' of my partner is converted to the ability to rejoice in our opposites when I learn to appreciate the complementarity which these differences bring out.

The untidy woman married to a meticulous mate, the aggressive driver married to a cautious road-user, the spendthrift married to a miser, are the subjects of jokes, comedies and novels. They also exist in real life and couples have to learn to come to terms with the personal habits of the partner.

When love is creative, at least two approaches present themselves to partners who are in conflict over personal habits. On the one hand, there is the need to accept your spouse as he/she is, with the particular habit which irritates you. The habit of the loved one is a part of him/her. But, when your favourite habit infuriates your partner, or when it originates from thoughtlessness, love of your spouse demands a change of behaviour. When two people approach the same problem with these attitudes, when they are able to communicate openly, satisfactory compromise nearly always suggests itself.

It is the same with clashes over life-style, when you both bring varying standards of living to your home-making. The willingness to lay aside cherished standards of living and behaviour patterns in the pursuit of a manner of life which is mutually satisfying is vital.

The same principles apply when discrepancies arise between married people in the way they communicate the message, 'I love you'. The romantic person is one who likes to communicate love through cuddles, kisses and red roses.

Some practical people express affection by washing-up, doing the shopping unexpectedly, filling the hot-water bottle. The romantic is tempted to overlook this love language, and to whine, 'you don't love me any more.' Each must learn to receive the love signals the other gives, to rejoice in them and to record them mentally and emotionally. Similarly each can learn to use the language of the other, perhaps awkwardly at first, but gradually finding it comfortable and natural. In this way couples avoid that destructive fear, the uncertainty which doubts love.

To sum up: *Do you find yourself reflected in this chapter so far? Where?*

What is there about your partner which is the opposite of yourself? How do you feel about that?

How can you encourage this 'otherness'?

Is your place of chief resource in Christ or your partner?

A strategy

I have tried to show in these two chapters that tension is to marriage what birth pangs are to childbirth. They are the unmistakable warnings that new life is forthcoming. They provide the motivation to strain every muscle and nerve to bring forth the life which is part of both of you. Healthy attitudes to conflict – the ability to understand its causes, the willingness to modify behaviour patterns, the respect of the 'otherness' of your partner, are antiseptics, preserving the new life. Positive action – the loyalty which binds you together, honest communiction, accurate listening to the undercurrent of love and appropriate application of the dynamic of Christian love (1 Cor. 13), are anti-toxins preventing disease destroying that which you create.

I want to underline that two highly motivated people, harnessed to their Creator-God, possess all the resources required to arrest the malaise of marital disharmony. The sustained centrality of the lordship of Christ in all, over all and through every aspect of marriage and the availability of the miracle-power of prayer provide you with an unlimited strategy in times of conflict.

Now it is over to you. I leave you with a project. On the

basis of the last chapter and this:

What plans are you plotting for those inevitable occasions when tension will assault your relationship?

What are your feelings when tension divides you?

What well-tried methods assure you that tension will give birth to something new and lovely?

How do you feel about the hard work involved in resolving tension?

C. S. Lewis once reflected on the tension which existed in his own marriage: 'The most precious gift that marriage gave me was this constant impact of something very close and intimate yet all the time unmistakably other, resistant – in a word, real.'[2]

Notes for chapter twelve

1. D. H. Lawrence, *The Rainbow* (Penguin, 1949), p.167.
2. C. S. Lewis, *A Grief Observed* (Faber, 1961), p.18.

13 Two More Growth Points: Inlaws and Money

In-laws

An elderly, hard-bitten man once described his tangled relationship with his daughter-in-law. He spoke of her with venom and the hatred of years. Some months later, his tone of voice had changed when he mentioned her. He seemed softer, almost loving. When I asked what had brought about his change of heart, he invited me to inspect the rose-bed she had weeded for him while he was bed-ridden. He waved his hand in the direction of the windows she had cleaned and showed me the tray, tastefully prepared for his afternoon tea. It was true that their views about almost everything clashed. But now there was an understanding between them. They no longer fought each other. They were 'for' each other.

Like the legendary mouse who gnawed away at the ropes which bound a man until the frayed edges snapped, this woman learned that persistent love really works. Love is patience personified. It is kindness incarnated in the middle of strife. It is shown by a person who never gives up working towards reconciliation. As Christians, we are to love our in-laws like that.

In-law conflict is not inevitable, of course. Some couples *like* their in-laws. Many appreciate the advice, practical support and prayer backing which in-laws readily give. When a woman develops a Naomi-Ruth friendship with her mother-in-law, both lives are enriched, and the husband's role is made easier. Christian couples have a twofold commission from God: to love, support and care for their parents (see Ex. 20:12; Lv. 20:9; 1 Tim. 5:8; Jas. 2:14–26) and to leave their parents and cleave to one another. The command is to love parents *and* each other, not to love parents *or* one another.

Some couples find no problem in fulfilling this divine command. They express mutual satisfaction as parental relationships deepen and friendships thrive. So when Dr Evelyn Duvall undertook to research into in-law problems, 25% of the study declined to comment. They were perfectly content with the developing relationships with their respective parents.

I recognize, however, that like the other 75%, you might have had something to say. Maybe your marital harmony is being disrupted by a mother-in-law who is over-protective of her son, by a father-in-law who feels you are not good enough to be grafted into the family tree, by a mother-in-law who attempts to control your marriage, insisting, albeit subtly, that things must be done her way. Or maybe you feel the pull of the pathetic parent figure who has failed to establish a close relationship with a spouse, who has lived life through you and who now feels the wrench of watching a part of his/her life slip away. You may have a parent who is a widow or widower or divorcee with deep loneliness problems.

All of us can find fault with others if we try, but I am assuming now that you have in-law problems and that you want to discover a way through them. I therefore propose that we look first at ourselves. And I shall put to you four specific questions:

Do you want harmonious relationships with your in-laws or are you conditioning yourself to friction? Music-hall jokes suggest that in-law problems are inevitable. The Bible explodes this theory. Remember Naomi and Ruth for example. If you really want wholesome friendships to develop, you will have to offer love without expecting any immediate returns. It will be your responsibility to react to criticism and aggressive behaviour, not in a retaliatory way, but with the kindness which gnaws through the vicious fetters of diseased communication.

When your mother-in-law attempts to control your marriage by compulsive giving or with overbearing advice, I invite you to ask yourself a second question:

What is it about you that rises to her bait? You cannot bear responsibility for your mother-in-law's actions. You can and must bear full responsibility for your own. You may discover that you are as insecure as she is, so when she hits out at you it is as painful to the emotions as knocking a broken finger is to the hand.

Then take an objective look at the situation. Examine your relationship and try to assess what your in-laws are trying to communicate to you:

What is the underlying message which the controlling mother-in-law or the pathetic mother-in-law is trying to get across? How does that make you feel about her?

A friend helped me to see the other side of the problem recently. She told me of the hollow feeling which blighted her life when she felt her son was marrying the wrong girl. She feared that he was being swept off his feet by erotic love, that he would not be happy and that her disapproval would so communicate itself that it would drive a wedge between them.

Fears for her son coincided with fears for herself. She was afraid of the menopause, afraid that the years ahead heralded only old age. She was disappointed, too, that she hadn't much energy these days.

The message she wanted to communicate to her son, 'I love you', came out heavily disguised every time. Her fear expressed itself in outbursts which more nearly resembled hatred than love. But then, hatred and love can be divided only by a very fine thread.

So my fourth question is:

What do you think motivates your mother-in-law's behaviour? Try to see life through her spectacles and accurately assess her emotional, financial and health needs. When you have done this, you can work out together how you might begin to meet those needs, bearing in mind your double calling. You are called to honour and serve your in-laws. You are required to nourish and cherish one another.

If you adopt certain attitudes, your in-laws will be incapable of driving a wedge between the two of you. Jesus gives us one clue with the reminder that a divided household is an easy target to those who are out to destroy. But a united household is impregnable. In other words, it is essential that you do not go home to mum and dad to complain about your partner. It is vital that you do not belittle one another in front of either set of parents. I am not saying that you should pretend that you never disagree. I am saying that loyalty is of the essence of enriched relationships.

Love produces more love. When a mother-in-law hears her son affirming his bride in front of her, the message is clear. Their love is intact, it is not to be violated. And it's a brave mother who consistently wages war under those circumstances!

Most parents enjoy and secretly hope for friendship with their adult children. 'It's the openness, the lovingness, the fact that they're so easy to talk to that makes it so good.' Friendship includes letting another in on some of your plans about the present and the future.

Young people are often impetuous and unrealistic in their expectations. Those do well who are prepared to hear the opinions of others, who are ready to weigh the advice of parents and humble enough to concede that it might contain a glimmer of the truth. I am not suggesting that it is your duty to accept all the advice you are given. I am saying that relationships are strengthened when you are generous enough to ventilate plans and choices with those who have watched your development for a good number of years. One young wife told me that she sometimes asks her husband's mother for advice even when she doesn't need it. It gives her mother-in-law a feeling of being wanted and deepens their friendship.

Kindness is the love which stands no nonsense. Kindness is the nurse who insists on jabbing her needle in a patient's arm to hasten his recovery. Kindness to in-laws is not sentimental. Kindness is setting realistic limitations so that you can enjoy realistic relationships. Parents, like friends, often hesitate to offer help and frequently appear to interfere because couples do not set clear boundaries. Love for your in-laws requires you to set the limits which will safeguard your embryonic relationship and at the same time upbuild your friendship with them. Christian love is then characterized by patience when they over step the mark and persistence in working for peaceable relations.

I offer a check-list which you might care to use from time to time:

1. *Are you, as husband and wife, consistently loyal to each other?*
2. *What are the boundaries you want to set your in-laws? time, discussing plans, seeking advice? When can they phone/visit? When is it inconvenient?*
3. *What kind of relationship would you like to develop with your in-laws?*
4. *What do you want from them? Prayer, advice, letters?*
5. *What can you give them?*
6. *What practical things can you do to keep the relationships in good working order?*
7. *Have you prayed for your in-laws recently?*
8. *Are you making a fuss of birthdays, anniversaries and special visits to communicate the message that you do care?*

Money

The claim is made that 50% of the marriages in the United States which collapse do so because money is mismanaged. Whether these figures are accurate or not, money matters constitute a major cause of the disruption of marital harmony in the western world. I propose to tackle the subject from a biblical point of view and to include some practical advice. Space is limited, so I recommend that you also read the appropriate sections in Mary Batchelor's book, *Getting Married in Church*,[1] David R. Mace's book, *Getting Ready for Marriage*,[2] and Simon Webley's booklet, *Money Matters*.[3]

What gives rise to this conflict? Why do Christians, just like other people, find it so easy to lose a clear perspective?

One reason is that Christian couples are bombarded by the persuasive voices of the media. The world's plausible message that the size of your pay-packet, the situation of the house you buy and the number of gadgets cluttering your home define your worth, is difficult to resist. Christians as well as materialists begin to believe that money is a status symbol. We are tempted to ignore the clear teaching of Christ who assures us that it is not what you have that counts. It is not the size of your bank balance which impresses Him, but how you choose to apportion it.

If you believe that wealth is a status symbol and if your expenditure has to be on a lower scale than you are accustomed to, you are in danger of falling into another trap. It is the feeling that you have every right to more. You feel insulted and ashamed and wallow in self-pity. But the Bible teaches Christians to be content with what they have and to resist the clamour for more. It exhorts us to give thanks for what God gives, and to exercise efficient stewardship of small amounts of money as well as large.

The media's three-fold claim sounds attractive: your money is yours, do what you like with it; believe all the advertisements; riches and possessions bring happiness. It is easy to forget that this claim is refuted in Christ's teaching. He shows us that possessions are a trust from God, that the love of wealth is the root of thorny problems and that, far from bringing fulfilment, possessions very frequently choke the word of God (Mk. 4:19; 1 Tim. 6:9–10).

Christian teaching emphasizes giving, not getting. It challenges us to give at least 10% of our income to God. And it places a heavy emphasis on good stewardship of the remaining 90%.

The persuasiveness of the media, the pressures of parents, the selfishness of personal instincts and the different standards which two people inevitably bring to the same marriage, give rise to friction and misunderstanding. It is therefore essential that two people who are building a life-long partnership should have an agreed policy over money.

The Bible's insistence that, as Christians, we are accountable to the Divine Treasurer for that which He entrusts to us cannot be ignored. That reason alone should push us into establishing an organized, systematic, responsible attitude to financial matters. The Chief Executive is God. The earthly treasurer might be the wife or the husband. Does it matter? What does matter is that you should settle for an agreed policy, allowing the one more adept at figures to deal with the practicalities.

If you are to agree about the way you spend your money, you each need to know the full extent of your income(s), assets and probable expenditure. To ensure that expenditure will not exceed income, it is helpful to draw up a budget placing known items(tax, insurance, mortgage payments, gas bills, electricity bills, *etc.*) alongside your income. Then balance the books. But for the Christian, budgeting will not be determined by wants. It will be resolved by needs. Decisions will be governed by the recognition of what you can do without. It will not be governed by what you must have to be like the neighbours, your parents or what you read in magazines. Even needs will be tooth-combed, placed within a global perspective, alongside neighbourhood needs and church needs. In other words, budgets will flow from a responsible, Christian, world-wide perspective and from prayer. They will not be the result of your latest whim or the most recent fashion.

This is not only biblical teaching, it is sound common sense. It puts an end to quarrels which arise from the mis-management of money and it gives you a firm base from which to meet the personal financial needs of the marriage.

Christ makes demands on our pockets. On those who are rich, and that includes all of us who live in the west, He makes demands. But God is no man's debtor. The same God, from the abundance of His resources, gives blessings. He has promised that this will continue (See 2 Ch. 31:3–10; Pr. 3:9–10; Acts 20:35).

Sometimes His reward comes in the form of financial provision which stuns us into silent praise. But the chief benefits transcend the poverty of riches. When you agree on a policy with one another and with Christ, you banish pretence, you introduce into your marriage the cheerfulness in giving which God so loves, you share a secret of which the world knows nothing and you have a purpose which unites you and increases your spiritual awareness. Christ turns our attitude to money upside down.

In traditional middle-class marriages, the husband was the wage earner. It was not uncommon for the wife to be ignorant of the size of his pay-packet. He would give her the housekeeping money. The rest he would pocket and he was unaccountable to anyone for the way it was spent. This practice frequently encouraged the wife in the under standable, though deceitful, practice of building a secret hoard from which she would buy presents and personal items and which gave her a feeling of independence.

Husbands at the lower end of the salary scale in traditional marriages handed the entire pay-packet to the wife and she extracted from the brown envelope his 'pocket-money'. She administered the money, distributing it in whatever way she chose. The first method was humiliating for the wife and the second degraded the husband.

In this book I have been emphasizing togetherness in marriage, with Christ, because I am excited by the concept of marriage as I believe God intends it to be – two people growing to understand one another, living in harmony for the glory of Christ's Kingdom.

In financial affairs, as in other matters, I am suggesting that we do not ignore the valuable insights of the world, but refuse to allow them to supplant the higher teaching of Christ through the inspired message of the Bible. I am proposing that you combine your financial resources so that two sources merge to become one. From that plentiful supply, comparatively speaking, I am suggesting that you apportion a pile of money for God, regularly, systematically, proportionate to His goodness to you and honestly (see 1 Cor. 8 and Acts 5:3). Then agree on an allowance for the needs of the marriage, tax, bills, car *etc*. Apportion a sum which covers personal needs, hair-cuts, talcum powder, after-shave, books and clothes, whatever you feel needs to go on the list. And learn to laugh about money!

These are some ways of approaching the financial problem, even in these days of high inflation. They result in purposeful living. Handling money is one more area which gives an opportunity to work together positively. It need not threaten our unity. Refer to this check-list from time to time:

1. *Are you prepared to face up to your financial boundaries or do you a. blame your partner, b. complain, c. indulge in self-pity because you are less wealthy than others?*
2. *Do you believe that God is no man's debtor? that He really does care?*
3. *What proportion of your income(s) goes to: God's work, to the marriage, to each partner? Review this distribution from time to time.*
4. *When you receive a rise do you a. give more away, b. buy unnecessary*

items, c. stake your personal claim to it?
5. *What can you do without so that the Kindgom of God might be extended and believers strengthened?*

Notes of chapter thirteen

1. Mary Batchelor, *Getting Married in Church* (Lion, 1979).
2. David R. Mace, *Getting Ready for Marriage* (Oliphants, 1974).
3. Simon Webley, *Money Matters* (IVP, 1978).

14 Entrusted with Suffering

I am glad that, when I received the telephone call which told me that my mother was critically ill, I had no idea that the pain of watching her last hours of suffering would be the first of a series of tragedies. I did not know then that a few months after my mother's death my brother would die, aged thirty-three. I was unaware that only weeks after that, a ginger-beer bottle would explode in my face involving me in a series of facial operations, none of them completely successful.

When we left England for a family holiday in Greece, just 'to catch our breath', we were unaware that our car would overturn in Yugoslavia. And we did not know that while we were on holiday my father would die. After all, he was a healthy, happy man when we left home. Even if we had known, we would have been unprepared for what followed: the troughs of depression, the feelings of near despair which tormented me from time to time and the darkness which would sometimes descend like a blanket, leaving me feeling very frightened. Each fresh blow took us by surprise and it was with difficulty that we learned to cope.

Others have spoken to me of their suffering. They have described some of the methods they stumbled upon which enabled them to deal with personal bereavement, physical pain and stressful situations. I believe I see a sort of pattern emerging and I have drawn on these findings of others in the hope that they might help you if God should choose to entrust your marriage with sorrow. This sorrow might come through redundancy, criticism or being hurt by others outside the marriage. But I use two major causes of suffering, illness

113

and bereavement, to examine some of the feelings people experience when the going is tough.

Fear

There is the panicky feeling, 'I can't cope', It is a feeling most people experience when life hurts and an admission which needs to be voiced. It often happens that, when you recognize that you can't cope, you discover an ingenious streak within yourself – the ability to seek out ways of overcoming suffering.

I think of one man who described how he felt when he first heard the news of his wife's incurable illness. 'The pain was intolerable. I felt plunged into something which was greater, more powerful than me. I found myself crying inwardly, "I can't cope".' Yet he found that immense strength seemed to be set free within himself. He found that his fears were ungrounded, that he could work all day and then stay up all night without becoming exhausted. It was as if he first needed to acknowledge his inadequacy, before God added to him the resources he needed to tread the pathway of sorrow with his wife.

I recall visiting a young mother and her new-born child in hospital. The baby was born with a ventricular hole in the heart. She had an oesophogeal reflex which would necessitate keeping her upright day and night. It seemed unlikely that she would keep her food down for long. As the husband walked from the ward to the hospital entrance with me, he confessed that he could not cope with a responsible lecturing post, a wife who must be totally absorbed in her sick baby, three other children *and* all the normal household chores. We recognized that his feelings were realistic. We acknowledged that this was where the support of the 'body of Christ' could find expression, and he began to think of people in the church who might be asked to help regularly. I admired that husband. He refused to pretend that all was well when it was not. He recognized where help was needed and was unafraid to ask for it. He carefully worked out his own scale of priorities in a stressful situation. It was a good example of the creativity of pain.

Our needs are not only practical ones, they are often deep-seated emotional ones. When our car was written off in

Yugoslavia, we had to travel across Europe by inter-continental rail. At that time I was unable to sit upright for long periods and I was still shocked by the impact of the accident. I remember trembling with fear, just like a little child, whenever David left me. Others have spoken to me of this fear and the childlikeness. 'When they mentioned the word cancer, I felt sick, frightened, incomplete. I felt aband-oned. I became like a little boy searching for his mother.'

The insights provided by psycho-analysts help us to understand this childlike behaviour. One theory is that each of us is capable of dealing with life, to use the jargon, either 'in the adult' or 'in the child'. The reason for this, it is suggested, is that within each adult lives a child who is still capable of jumping for joy, crying with pain or trembling with terror. In adverse circumstances, the adult sometimes loses control, and 'the child' takes over.

Monica Furlong emphasizes that in those times of stress, people need extra loving and cherishing. We need to learn to *love* ourselves!

> To love the self means...to pay attention to the real situation: the battered baby within each one of us who does need our care and our patience. It means refusing to condemn or punish ourselves, to find ourselves contemptible or disgusting, but on the contrary gentling ourselves along through all the ups and downs of existence with real charity of heart, finding ourselves touching, funny, in-teresting, attractive, as we would a real child.[1]

Dependency, petulance and fear are often cries for help. They are soothed by tenderness, understanding and patience. Just as it is both folly and cruelty to smack a hurt child, so we need to avoid blaming or punishing the weeping child within our partner or ourselves. Just as you would cuddle a real child you must find ways of expressing love to the suffering child who lives within an adult. I am not suggesting that you spoil 'the child' by giving in to unrealistic demands, whining or manipulation. That would be counter-productive. Nor am I saying that such a person is not a sinner in need of forgive-ness. I *am* saying that couples must cherish one another, especially during times of testing. To bottle up emotion and play the part of the tough, unyielding 'example to everyone' is storing up trouble for the future and is probably more the result of pride than of real nobility. Jesus did not say, 'When things are hard, put a brave face on it, stick it out.' He *did* say, 'Come to me, all of you who are tired from carrying heavy loads, and I will give you rest. Take my yoke and put it on you, and learn from me, because I am gentle and humble in spirit; and you will find rest. For the yoke I will give you is easy, and the load I will put on you is light' (Mt. 11:28–30 GNB). Bringing your load to Jesus often results in being humble enough to bring your load to someone else as well.

Sexual intercourse is also therapeutic. The problem with certain crises is that, at the very moment the partners need the consolation which sexual play frequently affords them, they are deprived of this source of comfort. As one man expressed it, 'When my wife reached the peak of her illness, I was hungry sexually. I felt so isolated and desperately wanted the completion which only a woman can bring.' It is vital at such times to listen to what your emotions are saying and to face the real situation with the Lord who has resources to meet you in the hollow of your distress.

For this reason it can be unkind and counter-productive to applaud one another for putting a brave face on it. People used to marvel at the serene way in which I was accepting each new loss, but they failed to recognize that my peaceful exterior was plastic and the day of reckoning with rebel emotions had to come.

Anger

Adverse circumstances often provoke anger. Anger is an uncomfortable feeling. It is as alive as an electric current, with all the potential to destroy as well as all the power to illuminate. We must not be afraid of anger. Rather, we must learn how to handle it. Repressed anger has physical consequences: high blood-pressure, hypertension, eczema, for example. There may be depression, insomnia or phobias of various kinds. 'Anger, like a baby, grows stronger when it is nursed.'[2]

But anger can be positive. In its proper place it is a necessary and healthy part of human nature. The Bible recognizes that the right use of anger has a place in the Christian's life: 'Be angry, but sin not' (Ps. 4:4).

One way to make anger work for you is to ventilate it. When aggression is driven down inside you it saps the energy you need to cope with crises. But when it is expressed, it earths your feelings, releases tension and sheds light on the reason for the ambivalence you feel. This leaves you free to act.

Jesus is our model for the effective use of anger. When He watched men cheat their brothers, defiling His Father's house, He was angry. He exposed the deceit, overturned the money-tables and evicted the money-lenders from the temple. He ventilated His anger, took action against those who wronged God, but He did not sin. We, too, sometimes need to react to evil.

There is a heresy which asks us to praise God for the evils which assault our lives. But Jesus did not condone evil. On the contrary, whenever He recognized the Evil One at work, He denounced Satan. Satan's activity provoked Him to anger. He was therefore unafraid to rebuke the evil at work in Peter: 'Get thee behind me Satan.' Like Jesus:

> we must look evil full in the face, see it for the unacceptable horror it is, dare to call it evil – also when it happens to us. For when nature assaults *my* life, it is no less an evil than when it assaults the life of a friend or loved one. A cancer in my own body is an evil just as it would be were it in my child's body. We must be as honest about evil when it attacks us as we are when it attacks others. It is *unacceptable,* plainly and completely. God does not want us to affirm the work of His enemy.[3]

One young wife learned to use anger when cancer cells threatened to dismember her body. On one occasion she wrote:

> I hate Satan because whilst I can almost bear him attacking me, when it comes to my husband and little girl being affected then I just feel very angry. I hate the illness which has robbed me of my youth, taking part of my husband's

also. I feel so angry but I haven't enough energy to express it except by sometimes writing.

I am not advocating an irresponsible mishandling of anger, where you explode whenever you feel like it. This could be very hurtful to other people. I am suggesting that the causes of your anger must be listened to, that you need to find an appropriate place to let it out and that it is an emotion which many people experience. Rightly handled, anger can provoke you into action, to overcome sorrow.

Stepping-stones

I hope you may never need this chapter, but if you do then you might find some of the following suggestions helpful. They are the stepping stones which others have used.

'With Christ is the key. I don't know how one copes without Him.' The man who said that to me went on to speak of the importance of the fellowship and support of the body of Christ. 'And yet we didn't pray much. Somehow we couldn't. There wasn't time for one thing. And there were no words. Others prayed, though, and the effect of their prayers was often tangible. I've never experienced anything like it before.'

The parents of a sick child expressed something similar: 'Hardly knowing what to pray ourselves, it was a source of tremendous comfort and relief to be told, "You look after your children and we'll bear the responsibility of praying".'

Prayer is one stepping-stone. The Christian couple has another. It is the guarantee of the presence of Christ in every situation. Someone described this stepping-stone in this way, 'Whatever comes to you next comes to you with God.' As Jesus said, 'I will not leave you desolate' (Jn. 14:18).

In times of loss, the actual loss through death of one you love, the threatened loss of a loved one who becomes ill, the emotional loss of cherished hopes, close personal relationships, possessions or your job, you need this assurance because you feel vulnerable. Most people react to loss by clinging to the past, demanding their 'rights', clasping their fingers around that which remains lest someone should prise the little they have left from their reluctant hands. But in the face of suffering we must learn to say goodbye to what might have been, the closeness, the friendship and fulfilment, so that we are free to receive the present and the future. We have to unclench our fists so that the past falls away, so that, with open palms, we may receive what God offers of peace, consolation and joy, in the present. This is the third stepping-stone.

The couple who found themselves, against all the contraceptive odds, with an unplanned child found no peace until they said a reluctant farewell to the higher standard of living and the longed-for freedom. When those goodbyes had been said, however, they saw beauty in their child, rediscovered love in one another and found joy in family life.

When you watch the 'might have beens' slip away, gradually you begin to receive the gift of the present, the gift of 'now', the fourth stepping-stone.

One man told me how he and his wife discovered the richness of 'now':

We were faced with one option, separation through death. We could no longer live in the future, planning our next summer or the cottage we would buy for our retirement. We couldn't even live in next week's diary; next week might not arrive for our partnership. We learned to receive each hour as a gift, asking 'What shall we read this morning?' 'How shall we enjoy the eternity of "now"?' We enjoyed the fullness of life, and our mutual sharing contained an eternal quality. I was aware of her. She was aware of me.

When you keep glancing over your shoulder to the past, regretting the loss of what might have been, the question which rises from deep within is 'Lord, why?' 'Why did he have to die now?' 'Why couldn't you have warned me?' 'Why...? Why...? Why...?' And the Christian must learn that there is no answer to the question 'Why?' But if you allow the past to remain in the past, if you learn to live in the immediacy of the present, then a new question is prompted, 'Lord, what do you want me to learn from this situation?' The comfort is that the second question 'Lord, *what*...?' has an answer and though the reply may be painful because the lessons to be learned are costly, there is that awareness deep down that you are moving forward, you are progressing into the present with God.

Then the valley of weeping does become a place of springs where pools of blessing and refreshment collect after the rain (see Ps. 84).

For it is the experience of many that 'God prepares a hospital for those He has to wound,' or, more accurately, 'God prepares a hospital for those who require His surgery.' The cutting edge of the surgeon's scalpel dissects so that the skilled hands might repair, make good that which is broken and make whole that which is diseased. Suffering is the pathway to healing. As someone once said to me during our troubled years, 'How much God must love you to entrust you with so much sorrow.'

As married people we do not have to cope with crises on our own. We are in them together. At such times, as one husband expressed it, 'It's not what you *do* but what you *are* that matters. Is this only a trite cliché? I don't think so. You need to be there, to listen, all night if need be, to be a channel for the love of God, to understand, (even when you are being told that you couldn't possibly understand).'

This kind of support provided a stepping-stone for this man's wife. It enabled her to climb out of depression. 'It would be an awesome thing to say that we are grateful for such an experience, but our love for and closeness to each other has moved into a higher gear than ever before.'

When one partner suffers, both suffer. It is the acme of togetherness. Henri Nouwen describes the cost of this love: 'Those who do not run away from our pains but touch them with compassion bring healing and new strength. The paradox indeed is that the beginning of healing is in the solidarity with the pain.'[4]

This chapter may make little sense to those who have never worked through personal suffering. But I include it with the hope that it may help you to understand your reactions should you encounter life's hurts. Perhaps it will help you to understand what other couples are facing:

Do you know of anyone who is being entrusted with sorrow at the moment?

Could you undertake to 'be the pray-er' for them while they undertake the hard work of living?

Is there practical help you could offer?

Are you able to help them to understand their emotions by listening, feeding back to them what they seem to be feeling and praying so that they will know that they are being wounded for life and not spiritual death?

Notes for chapter fourteen

1. Monica Furlong, *Christian Uncertainties* (Hodder and Stoughton, 1975), p.15.
2. *Be angry and sin not* (Care and Counsel, Pamphlet No.2, 1980).
3. Lewis Smedes, *Love within limits* (Lion, 1979), p.16.
4. Henri Nouwen, *Reaching out* (Fount, 1976), p.60.

15 God Goes About Mending Broken Things

Some years ago, an Oxfam poster portrayed a starving, pot-bellied, African child talking to his weary hollow-eyed mother. The child was asking a question, 'Mother, what does God do all day?' The emaciated woman was replying, 'God, my son, goes about all day mending broken things.'

Jane loved to recall her wedding day. It had been a fitting climax to all she and John had planned during all those months of engagement. On that day they had dedicated themselves and their marriage to God, and life seemed to be unfolding before them in an exciting way. Then there had been the long summer holidays. How she and John had enjoyed decorating the house, attending to the garden and finding homes for the wedding presents!

September came and John resumed his teaching job. The Crusader Class started up again and he loved his Sunday afternoons with the boys. Gradually John's friends began to drop in to see them. And John, fulfilled in his job, happy with his Christian activities, secure in the friends around him, used to whistle as he walked from the station in the evenings. He enjoyed being married.

Jane too began her teaching job in September. But the area was new to her. Shopping seemed to take a long time because she hadn't yet found her way around without John. And John's church seemed strange with all those unfamiliar people to meet. Of course, Jane enjoyed meeting John's friends but she found herself missing her own companions from college days and her relatives seemed miles away.

The staff at Jane's school were very friendly. They were

kind and showed her the way they did things. But they had all been there for years and had formed their staff-room cliques. Jane sometimes felt a complete outsider in the staff-room.

Whenever she dared to peep inside at her feelings, she felt an outsider everywhere; in the neighbourhood, at church, among John's friends and at school. And John continued to whistle as he walked up from the station. He sang in his bath and he hummed as he washed up. He was so happy that he failed to notice his bride's loneliness.

At school, Jane used to watch Ron. He was a Christian for one thing, an excellent teacher for another, and it interested her that whenever the children had problems, they talked to him. He was the one who would move out of the cliques to befriend her in the staff-room. Gradually, she found herself unburdening her troubles to him. She always felt better after they had talked and she assured herself that it was quite safe. After all he was twenty years older than she.

Jane used to thank God for Ron. Their growing friendship felt so right. He understood her and sometimes she felt that his companionship was the only thing which prevented her from caving in.

Driving to school one morning, she could not deny the feelings of excitement which the thought of Ron aroused. She knew she was looking forward to seeing him in the same way that she used to look forward to seeing John when they were engaged. Was she falling in love with Ron? She couldn't be. She was married to John. The marriage was only three months old.

But when Jane became obsessed with fantasies about sleeping with Ron and when she imagined herself making love to Ron while she lay in John's arms, she knew that an emotion too powerful for her was sweeping her off her feet. And she did not know how to cope. What she did know was that Ron was beginning to feel the same way.

Should she stop seeing him? That was impossible since they worked together. Should she sleep with Ron? Her loyalty to John and her Christian principles would not permit that. Should she leave John and marry Ron? But she loved John deeply and didn't want to hurt him. Suddenly Jane seemed to be 'cornered' by pain.

The way in which Jane and Ron severed their attachment to one another, the confession Jane made to John and the generous way in which John reacted, would take pages to relate. Instead of dwelling on those details, I propose to focus on the reconciliation which took place between John and Jane. I have mentioned this true story because I believe we need to be aware that these things do happen. They happen to Christians. They almost always happen for one reason. When emotional needs are not met within marriage, the deprived partner deliberately, or unconsciously, searches for help elsewhere.

I have included some of the details of the distress encountered by John and Jane because their marriage eventually emerged from a kind of dying to a kind of resurrection. Their experience illustrates that God does go about mending things, including splintered marriages.

Acceptance

The rebuilding of a marriage is not instantaneous. It is not the triumphalistic waving of a wand which rights all wrongs. On the contrary, it is a slow, painful process which suffers setbacks as well as steps forward. Neither Jane nor John had wanted to hurt each other. But then, couples who marry one another rarely do. They were astonished that each was able to inflict such deep emotional wounds on the other. They learned, through the bitterness of experience, that married love is fragile. It needs to be constantly renewed, continually rediscovered. The realization that adult persons have basic personality needs which, when met, promote growth and become instruments of healing, was new to them. Neither had they discovered that when those basic needs are denied, persons crumble. No-one can blame them for that lack of information. They were unaware of the ingredients which are essential to the sustenance of healthy marriages.

But the research of psychologists and psycho-analysts has increased our understanding and knowledge of the hunger-needs of persons. Their insights emphasize the importance of the role of the spouse in attempting to meet those needs.

There is the basic need all persons have to be accepted just as they are. Acceptance does not mean merely making a place for a person in your pew. Acceptance is not given when you begin to create a life with someone and then go off at a tangent in the pursuit of self-fulfilment. Accepting persons involves making a place for them within yourself, carving out time for them, meeting their unexpressed but deeply felt needs *at cost to yourself*. Acceptance is not condoning all they do or agreeing with all they say. Acceptance without acquiescence is the goal. It means receiving a person to yourself, offering the security which creates the free and fearless space in which he/she may develop.

Accepting love is unconditional love. Unconditional love, *agapé*, 'forgives the guilty spouse, affirms the unlovely spouse, bears with bad taste, insensitive neglect, stupid decisions and cruel aggressiveness'.[1] And as John Powell rightly says, unconditional love is the only kind of love which enables persons to change and grow.

Forgiveness

Acceptance includes forgiveness; the forgiveness which feels the full brunt of the pain inflicted by the loved one but which, at the same time, continues to love the very person who has caused the injury.

But this is not the gospel of psychiatry. It is the good news which the Bible proclaims. In fact we find this kind of love modelled for us by God. In human terms it is described in Luke 15 where God is likened to a loving father who runs to greet his rebellious son, who flings his arms around the filthy youth, who so loves that he reclothes and reinstates the one who had thrown love back in his face.

On the Friday night when Jane confessed to John the details of her emotional entanglement with Ron, there was no flash of inspiration which enabled them to see what had been lacking in their marriage. They didn't even 'fall in love' all over again. Like two battered people they bumbled into an understanding of one another which they had not experienced before. But even that was gradual.

Their forgiveness of one another was generous. But it did not instantly cure John's insensitivity nor Jane's insecurity.

And even now they have to forgive over and over again. But their genuine love for one another rose above their failures. This drew them closer together.

They began to realize the importance of spending time together. When they were engaged, no matter how busy each of them had been, time together was a priority. Somehow, since their marriage, when term began, church activities started up again and friends were around, time seemed to elude them. They began to see that creating time for the other after you are married communicates the vital message that you value one another, you want your marriage to grow.

John didn't carefully analyse Jane's needs. He wouldn't have known how to, for one thing, and it wasn't his way. But because he loved her and desired her happiness, he began to express appreciation of the way she looked after their home. He admired the clothes she wore and spoke approvingly of her cooking. He showed interest in her class at school and they sometimes prepared lessons together. Gradually, Jane began to feel a person again. Her love for John was slowly reawakened. She would put it down to one word, 'love'. Psycho-analysts would define that over-simplified and mis-understood word with complex, though important, insights. It is sufficient for our study to recognize that love in marriage receives another unconditionally. Love forgives unfailingly It finds ways of expressing approval. It is perpetuated by giving another a sense of worth. It is the love which rescues persons from despair and loneliness. It is the love which heals the wounds of a life-time.

Hope

John and Jane felt battered for a long time. But that poster claims that *God* goes about mending broken things. Some-where deep within them, they discovered a response to that familiar statement of faith. In the past they had experienced its authenticity in their own lives. So they invited the God of love into the mangled mess of their marriage.

This God is a creative God. It was He who brooded over darkness and emptiness and created light, life, beauty and delicacy. His activity is also re-creative. He is the potter whose skilled and sensitive hands reshape persons, nations and relationships. God is a God of involvement. By becoming God incarnate, God tangible, God-with-us, He demonstrates that He is the God who descends into our lives. The baby born in Bethlehem speaks to us of a God who wants to be found, touched, handled, seen and heard in the midst of life's hurts. We can therefore focus on wholeness in the midst of brokenness.

It was as John and Jane submitted their brokenness to the re-creative power of God that they rediscovered that God mends broken things. They are still finding out for themselves that healing comes from God and through one another.

I often think of John and Jane and others like them when I am walking in Derbyshire. On the side of a hill, half-hidden by towering pine trees, there lies an undulating expanse of land. At one time it was laid waste. But now, if you go there in spring, you will find a landscaped garden ablaze with flamboyant colour – crimsons, reds, pinks, vermilions, purples, oranges, greens, browns and pure white. You can wander along the paths between the matured rhododendron bushes. You will see the primulas, narcissi and alpine rock plants. You can sit by a shaded pond in peace, enjoying the miracle.

A humble plaque explains how the miracle came about:

Beginning in 1935, at the age of 68, John Marsden-Smedley transformed this one-time quarry into the sheltered garden needed for rhododendrons. The making of this garden gave him and others many happy hours during the remaining 24 years of his life.

Lea rhododendron gardens speak of hope. They remind us of the value of co-operation. They show us the rewards of hard work. They help us to believe that couples co-operating with a re-creative God find relationships flourishing in the same way as flowers blossom on wasted land. This message, that the hard work of marriage reaps rich rewards, alleviates aloneness, and heals life's scars; this belief that the excitement of marriage consists as much in anticipating as in having, is the good news we have to spread. The good news about marriage is that, with Christ, two into one will go.

Notes for chapter fifteen

1. Lewis Smedes, *Love within limits* (Lion, 1979), p.101.